DESIGN MATTERS //

BROCHURES[01]

AN ESSENTIAL PRIMER FOR TODAY'S COMPETITIVE MARKET   MICHELLE TAUTE

ROCKPORT

First published in the United States of America by
Rockport Publishers, a member of
Quayside Publishing Group
100 Cummings Center
Suite 406-L
Beverly, Massachusetts 01915-6101
Telephone: (978) 282-9590
Fax: (978) 283-2742
www.rockpub.com

Library of Congress Cataloging-in-Publication Data

Taute, Michelle.
  Design matters, brochures : an essential primer for today's competitive market / Michelle Taute.
    p. cm.
  ISBN 1-59253-398-1
  1. Pamphlets--Design. 2. Graphic design (Typography) I. Title.
  Z246.T38 2008
  686.2'252--dc22

                                                    2007021208
                                                    CIP

ISBN-13: 978-1-59253-398-5
ISBN-10: 1-59253-398-1

10 9 8 7 6 5 4 3 2 1

Series Design: CAPSULE
Cover Design: CAPUSLE
Layout: Megan Cooney

Printed in China

Contents

INTROD

UCTION

"BROCHURES ARE ONE OF PRINT DESIGN'S MOST DELIGHTFUL AVATARS."
—DIVYA THAKUR, CREATIVE DIRECTOR AT DESIGN TEMPLE

WITH SO MANY MESSAGES COMING AT US EVERYDAY, BROCHURES HAVE BLENDED INTO OUR LIVES LIKE CAMOUFLAGE. THEY SHOW UP IN THE MAILBOX ALONGSIDE BILLS AND CREDIT CARD OFFERS. ONE MIGHT EVEN LAND ON YOUR DESK AT WORK TOUTING CHANGES IN HEALTH OR RETIREMENT BENEFITS. MAYBE A FEW MAKE THEIR WAY INTO YOUR HOUSE VIA YOUR CHILD'S BACKPACK. THEY COME WITH NEW GYM MEMBERSHIPS, NEW CAR SHOPPING, AND NEW ACHES AND PAINS.

Brochure Invasion

Racks of them vie for attention in hotel lobbies. In fact, you probably run across so many brochures in a week that you've stopped noticing the majority of them.

This competitive landscape may sound grim, but it also represents an opportunity. With the right message and a compelling design, you can help your clients cut through the clutter. Even the most brochure-weary eyes—those belonging to tired tradeshow frequenters—can be won over with a good solution. Maybe it's an innovative fold, unusual size, or emotional headline. It all depends on what's appropriate for the brand and problem at hand. Do you need to tell someone about a new product? Or build brand awareness? Is there an action you want readers to take after interacting with the piece?

And then there's the most important question of all: is a brochure the right solution? You've probably sat in a meeting in which a client exclaimed, "We need a brochure." Maybe you nodded your head in agreement or rolled your eyes as soon as you walked out the door. Some marketing departments seem to order up brochures just to look busy. It's your job to dig deeper to find the real problem: what do they want to accomplish? Then work with the client to find the best vehicle to turn those goals into reality—whether it's a website, poster, or brochure. It's key to speak up and present yourself as a true partner.

This book features head-turning brochures from top designers and firms around the world. You'll find everything from annual reports and retail brochures to paper promos and real estate pieces. After taking in the details, you can read up on how and why these pieces are effective print collateral. You'll glean tips, tricks, and best practices for everything from designing on a budget to wrangling celebrities for a photo shoot. Learn why a font or fold works so well for a particular piece. And understand the thought process and problem-solving approach that led to a gripping concept. Read on for inspiration, ideas, strategies, and solutions—information you can put to work on your next project.

MIND YOUR MANNERS

Since Washington, D.C., is the land of parties and fundraisers, it seemed only natural to play off the concept of an etiquette book to promote one of the city's upscale lifestyle stores. Muléh, the retailer in question, had recently added clothing to its existing furniture offerings, so it needed to promote this addition to customers. Plus the store wanted to expand its reach well beyond the surrounding city neighborhood.

▼ *This Modern Etiquette brochure promotes a lifestyle store called Muléh. Since the interior is so image-heavy, Design Army decided to keep the cover simple. The firm chose to print the piece on uncoated stock to complement the fact that most of the store's products are made from natural materials.*

So the team at Design Army set about putting a twist on old-fashioned manners. "How can we make it modern?" says Pum Lefebure, a creative director at the Washington, D.C., design firm. The answer: sprinkle a little humor throughout the copy and photographs. Next to rule No. 1—be fashionably on time—there is a picture of a woman wearing perfect clothes and makeup but still wearing hair curlers. Another essential guest rule—feet off the furniture—appears next to a photo of a woman lying on her back across a chair and ottoman with her legs and feet pointing straight in the air. As the fine print explains, "mankind left the caves for a reason."

These surprises keep readers engaged, but the design team was careful not to let the concept overshadow the store's merchandise. "We know how important it is to really focus on the product," Lefebure says. "The photographs must make you want to buy." Background colors, for example, were picked to enhance the furniture and clothing shown in each shot. Plus, these lust-worthy objects are clearly shown in the photographs. There's nothing in the image that prevents you from admiring a stylish purse or coveting an exquisite dining room table.

The design team did so much advance planning for the photo shoot that they were able to capture all nine images in a single day. Each shot was sketched out to give the photographer a visual blueprint, and Lefebure even sent the brochure's text to the modeling agency to familiarize them with the concept. The firm also briefed the hair and makeup person on the desired look and style, and planned the day so hair and make-up changes took place every other shot. After all, proper planning is the next best thing to impeccable manners.

Around the World

This book is an around-the-world tour in 200-plus brochures. The work found on these pages spans multiple continents, languages, and design philosophies. Though you can't necessarily pinpoint a specific geographic region by visual style, there are often bold shifts in approach from country to country. Many of these differences lie beneath the surface—you might not notice them looking at the finished work. But each one represents an opportunity to learn from a perspective different than your own.

At Studio Rašic in Croatia, the design team talks about their work with the ferocity and passion of painters. "We work the best when clients don't interfere in the design," says designer Marko Rasic. "That is when we have the freedom to work without compromises." For instance, a catalog the firm created for sculptor Petar Barisic falls into this category. He gave the design team the space and autonomy to execute the design to the best of their ability. After Studio Rašic completes an impressive piece like this, they often hear a familiar refrain from other clients: "Why don't you do something like this for us?"

In the United States, there tends to be more emphasis on collaborating with the client. Tamara Dowd, a creative director at Hirshorn Zuckerman Design Group (HZDG) in Rockville, Maryland, says young designers often struggle to learn that the client and job are bigger than their personal creativity. "It's not about you necessarily," she says. "You bring a lot of yourself to the plate, but you have to learn to adopt the appropriate style." A typical brochure project is about finding the right solution for the job rather than expressing a designer's personal style. A brochure with flashy paper and production qualities, for instance, probably sends the wrong message if the client is a small nonprofit.

Divya Thakur, a creative director at Design Temple in Mumbai, India, sums up the brochure design problem like this: "Brochures are one of print design's most delightful avatars. They speak to a captive audience and allow you the luxury of both space and time to communicate and impress the consumer." Depending on the particular audience, however, you may not be able to count on the luxury of time. Some brochures get tossed in the trash—or stuffed in a file folder—after a few seconds. But an appropriate message and delivery can carve out precious minutes from even the busiest schedule.

◄▼ To make this flipbook for Actia—a Paris-based organization that coordinates food industry research—graphic designer Anne-Lise Dermenghem started with the company's full logo and gradually made the tree smaller and smaller. She did a test flip every 10 pages and ended up with 64 separate images.

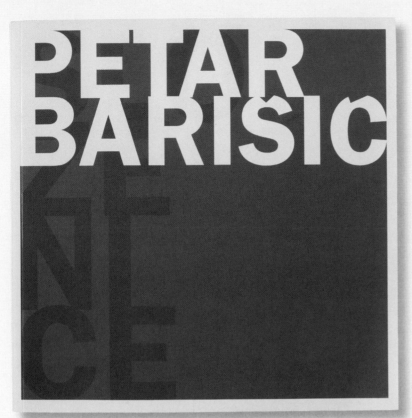

◄▼ *Croatian design firm Studio Rašic took design cues from this brochure's subject— sculptor Petar Barisic. The piece's type, for example, mimics the construction methods of the artist's works.*

Telling a Story

Brochures present a storytelling challenge. They're like miniature books in which you get to spin a tale with words and images. Will your brochure be reminiscent of a coffee table book? Or read more like a well-presented technical manual? From the trim size to the fold and the paper, there are almost endless possibilities to create a format that enhances the overall message—one that makes people stop and hold the piece in their hands or spend a few minutes skimming through the pages.

Since the messaging is just as important as the design, the first step is generally figuring out what story needs to be told. What is most important for people to come away with after glancing at the piece? How will you order this information? It is crucial to think about pacing and information hierarchy. What is the most interesting way to unfold the story? How can you draw people in and keep them turning the pages? Even the most gorgeous piece will fail if it doesn't get the right message across.

"The most difficult part of any brochure is figuring out consistent pacing while letting each spread be interesting," says Mike Mates, a lead designer at urbanINFLUENCE design studio in Seattle, Washington. If there's too much repetition, a piece becomes boring, but if the spreads don't hang together at all, it seems disjointed. One tactic he sometimes employs, for example, is formatting the text in a similar way—say, a head followed by a few sentences—and moving this copy block from spread to spread. "It's about establishing hierarchies and sticking to it," he says.

As Travis Cain, senior designer at Planet Propaganda in Madison, Wisconsin, points out, novice designers often struggle with long-form copy pieces. Many creatives fresh out of school simply haven't had a lot of experience working on them. Suddenly, they're faced with figuring out how to unfold a story with type and images over multiple pages. It presents a much different challenge than a poster or a business card. Cain is a fan of roughly mapping out a piece. He figures out where different text and images will go and how the story will unfold then goes back to refine it. It's a process that becomes easier with time and experience.

► *Before she designed this technical book, Paris-based designer Anne-Lise Dermenghem talked with the authors to make sure she understood the scientific text. She also worked with the writers to make sure the copy was organized in a clear way.*

Accutec™ Graters

Cuisipro.

Recipes inside.

▲► *Hahn Smith Design created this brochure to introduce a new line of high-end kitchen graters. "We wanted to show what the product looked like and how it worked," says Nigel Smith, a principal at the Toronto firm.*

Fresher flavour.

Other graters are dull and tear food, diminishing the flavour. Cuisipro® graters are better because our razor-sharp Accutec™ blades virtually glide through food, preserving its fresh flavour. It's all about taste.

Citrus Custard Tarts.

Makes 24 tarts. Preheat oven to 140°C/Gas mark 1. Place baked tart shells on a baking tray and set aside.

Place milk, grated citrus zest and vanilla extract in a saucepan and bring to a simmer over a low heat for 5 minutes. Remove from heat and allow to cool to infuse flavours. Meanwhile, in a separate bowl, blend eggs and sugar with a Cuisipro® silicone whisk. Continue whisking while gradually adding the milk. Pour filling into prepared shells and bake for 20 minutes or until filling is just set. Allow tarts to cool. Serve garnished with citrus zest and a dusting of icing sugar.

Ingredients
24 2-inch (5 cm) pre-baked
shortcrust pastry tart cases
500 mls whole milk
4 tbsp grated citrus zest (lemon,
lime or orange) plus extra for
garnish* (Grate using the Accutec™
fine grater)
6 eggs
4 tbsp caster sugar
1 tsp (5 mls) pure vanilla extract
Icing sugar to dust

*Grating tip: when using the Accutec™ fine grater to zest citrus fruits, be sure to make only one pass across the grater to avoid zesting the bitter white pith.

Q&A: MADAME PARIS

Sandrine Pelletier and Alexandra Ruiz formed Madame Paris in 2004; they describe the partnership as a "multifunctional robot." In more practical terms, the duo creates everything from art exhibitions to window displays and installations—the latter for fashion designers and brands. It's a long-distance creative relationship, with Pelletier based in Paris, and Ruiz in Geneva. Ruiz designed this piece, This Book was Made for my Cat Figaro, to highlight Pelletier's work from 2002 to 2006. "This is Sandrine Pelletier's first monograph disguised as a brochure," Ruiz says.

WHAT WAS THE DRIVING CONCEPT FOR THE DESIGN?

RUIZ: The design was to be simple. There are chapters for each period of work and the entrance to each chapter is a full-page image on top of another image (the one that will be at the beginning of the next chapter). These layers emphasize the intricateness of Sandrine's works. Each piece sinks into another.

HOW DID YOU COME UP WITH THE TITLE?

RUIZ: I knew Sandrine and I didn't want something too grand and snobby as a title, so the idea of making a book for Sandrine's cat was a way to pay homage to him and desacralize the artist's monograph.

PELLETIER: We were looking for something not too serious or pretentious. How I laughed when I saw the title. We both agreed on that title straight away.

TELL ME ABOUT THE COVER TYPOGRAPHY.

RUIZ: We wanted an old-fashioned, big black font, like an old American building; like someone you can trust and that is loyal; like history you cannot doubt. The use of caps is to bring the idea of something big and assertive.

▶ *Sometimes simple is best. This monograph presents Sandrine Pelletier's artwork in chronological order. Besides dates and titles, these images run without any explanatory text—an approach that keeps the emphasis on the artwork. There's additional information about Pelletier's work in the back of the book for readers who want to learn more.*

THIS BOOK WAS MADE FOR MY CAT FIGARO

BY SANDRINE PELLETIER

CAN YOU TELL ME ABOUT THIS COVER ILLUSTRATION? IS THAT REALLY FIGARO? IS HE STILL LIVING?

PELLETIER: Figaro was a black-and-white, obese cat. He was meowing like a castrato and was very, very special. His attitude was a source of inspiration for me in many ways. He was also very sweet, and funny, and I miss him a lot, as he died eight years ago.

RUIZ: The cat is like a mascot to Madame Paris.

WHAT WAS THE OVERALL DESIGN CONCEPT FOR THE BOOK? WHY SUCH A SIMPLE PRESENTATION?

RUIZ: I think it is important to maintain a book as an object, but not to pollute the artist's work with graphic details that might be unnecessary or decorative. The form serves the function and not the opposite.

WHY COVER THE BOOK IN PLASTIC?

PELLETIER: The plastic cover was added as a protective element, such as with library books, and also because it was printed in black and fragile to handle.

WAS THIS PRINTED PROFESSIONALLY OR ASSEMBLED BY HAND? OR IS JUST THE PLASTIC COVER DONE BY HAND?

PELLETIER: Just the plastic. One by one.

RUIZ: Everything is professional (laughs). The plastic part was done by hand, but the rest was printed on a press.

WHY SAVE ALL THE TEXT FOR THE BACK OF THE BOOK?

RUIZ: The book is a visual story. The text serves as complementary information. I like this way of seeing things. It's like a riddle. First, you try to understand or solve the problem on your own; then you go to the back to get the solution!

WHY DID YOU INCLUDE THE BRIGHT PINK END PAPERS?

RUIZ: It is like a hot shower in the morning: you wake up and then you are ready to jump into things.

PLANN

NG

"COME AT THESE PROJECTS FROM THE STANDPOINT OF BEING AN ADVOCATE AND A PARTNER—NOT AN AUTHORITY. YOU DON'T EVER WANT TO TALK DOWN TO YOUR CLIENT." —CHRISTIAN HELMS, A PARTNER AT THE DECODER RING

IT'S TEMPTING TO HEAD STRAIGHT FOR
THE COMPUTER OR SKETCHBOOK WHEN A
BROCHURE PROJECT HITS YOUR RADAR SCREEN.
BUT JUMPING AHEAD TO THE PIECE'S LOOK AND
FEEL BEFORE YOU TRULY UNDERSTAND THE
PROBLEM—AND HOW BEST TO SOLVE IT—ONLY
MAKES MORE WORK IN THE LONG RUN.

Building a Foundation

"The visual part is fun," says Thomas Hull, a principal at Rigsby Hull in Houston. "You want to cut right to the chase quickly." Taking the time to plan, however, is one of the most crucial stages of any successful project. Without knowing exactly what you're trying to achieve, it's nearly impossible to come up with an appropriate solution. So, where do you start if it's not at the keyboard? Ben Graham, a principal at Turnstyle in Seattle, believes there are three things you need to understand right away:

1. The client: do you know who the company really is and what challenges it faces?

2. The target audience: whom does your client want to reach and what will this group find compelling?

3. The relationship between the two: what will be believable to the audience?

These three knowledge points provide the foundation for working on any project, and if you want to truly understand each one, you'll need to spend some quality time getting to know your client. When Tim Hartford, president of Hartford Design in Chicago works with a new company, his team sits down with the key players and goes through a list of important questions. They'll ask about the business, target audience, and competition. Most clients can provide fairly detailed information about all three. Also, asking for samples of the company's existing materials offers further insight.

RbK

women

a few simple beliefs

▲► *Understanding the audience is a key part of planning any brochure. This piece, for example, was created to communicate with several groups: department-store buyers, fashion experts, and internal Reebok staff. "Overall, I think the feeling is somewhat soft and feminine," says Ben Graham, a principal at Turnstyle. "But it's not floral or dainty."*

We **believe** in a thousand shades of strong.

For women, strength comes in many forms. Not just the might and muscle kind of strong. Or the in-your-face kind of strong. But the kind of strong that's quiet. That's personal. That starts inside and works its way out. Above all, we believe in strength defined by courage—whether it's athletic courage, mental courage, or simply the courage of our convictions.

We believe in the brand called you.

Some brands need to own the spotlight. They command you to do it, be it, reach it—or else. Which begs the question: whose brand are we talking about anyway? We believe women care about brands, but they don't necessarily want to be a billboard for corporate aspirations. At Reebok, we're honored to play a supporting role in the starring attraction called you.

It also helps to conduct a little initial research of your own—even if it's just visiting the company's website—so you can ask more educated questions. "Try to learn as much as you can about the client and what their needs are," Hartford says. "That may even change what is delivered. They may have a preconceived notion that they need a website, but one of your questions may find that a direct-mail campaign really makes more sense."

Hartford recommends heading into the first client meeting with a blank slate and a willingness to listen. As the discussion progresses, try to hit all the essential questions. What differentiates the company from the competition? What messages would the client like to convey? Where would the company like to be in three to five years? What kinds of messages resonate with its audiences? Once you start to achieve a clearer picture of the company and audience, you can start to pare down the information. Hartford sums it up with this question: "If someone just walked away with one key message, what would it be?"

Eventually, the conversation should turn back to the project at hand. "What is it we want people to do as a result of that piece?" Graham

says. "Or is it just something they want them to think or feel about the company?" It's also crucial to know how the brochure will be used. Is it going to be given out on sales calls? Or mailed? Hull's firm takes the time to create a written summary—roughly a third of a page—outlining the message, who it's from, and who's going to receive it. "Once you have that clear in your mind, the content informs how it's going to look," he says.

▲◄ *It's important to know what a brochure needs to achieve. In this piece, Hartford Design helped position the Metaphase Design Group as the leader in handheld product research, ergonomics, and design. One way they accomplished this was by making the piece tactile. The push button on the cover, for example, is embossed.*

PULL
TWIST
GRIP
PINCH
MOVE
STEER
HOLD
SQUEEZE
TURN
TOUCH
LIFT
SLIDE
TIGHTEN
TAP
BEND
OPEN

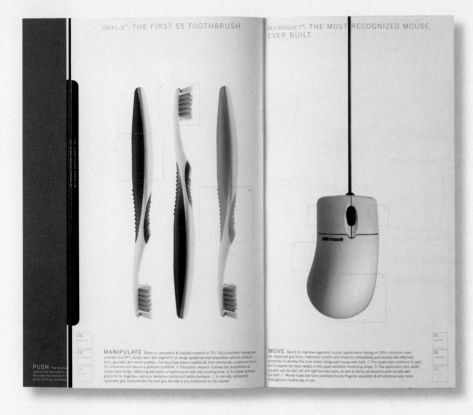

Communicating with Visual Cues

The team at Hahn Smith Design in Toronto approaches these early stages as an opportunity to build relationships and truly partner with clients. To foster better communication, they sometimes use visual cues. "Words like bold, or beautiful, or elegant, or modern—everyone has a very different interpretation of what they mean," says Nigel Smith, a principal at the firm. In order to get everyone on the same page, they might ask clients to bring actual objects they like or dislike to a meeting.

By helping designers get a handle on style preferences, this visual shorthand can move the conversation forward better than vague descriptors. One client, for example, presented Hahn Smith with a collection of items ranging from an architecture book and note cards to photos and artwork. "The client was saying, 'I want my stationery to fit in with this group of other things,'" Smith says. "It was a very proactive way of communicating." In the retail world, Hahn Smith might ask clients extremely direct questions such as, do you like the Gap logo or the Macy's logo? The responses provide them with feedback on style, color, and type, and help build the relationship.

Hands-on Research

Though talking with clients typically unearths a wealth of information, there's also something to be said for hands-on research. When Hahn Smith started working with the flatware company Gourmet Settings, for example, they did a lot of deliberate exploration into the context in which the product was sold. The team organized what they refer to as a "Happy Tour," renting a van and driving to Buffalo, New York, with the president of Gourmet Settings. The group spent the day visiting retailers and taking a look at how silverware is sold on store shelves.

▲► *Hahn Smith created this identical brochure in two sizes; the larger one goes to buyers, while the smaller version is included in every box of silverware. The woman holding the heart inside the front cover is actually Gourmet Setting's president. Since Hahn Smith has such a friendly relationship with her, they're truly able to partner on projects.*

We Care.

Every day our customers write us letters or send us e-mails raving about our flatware. These letters mean so much to us because they speak to our passion. They show us that we've made a connection with what we're doing and what you want. We're invited into homes to meet family and friends and we're honoured. Really.

Hildy Abrams, President

Nous sommes à l'écoute.

Tous les jours, les clients nous écrivent des lettres et nous envoient des courriels pour vanter nos couverts. Ces lettres veulent tout dire pour nous parce qu'elles témoignent de notre passion. Elles nous démontrent que nous avons établi un lien entre ce que nous faisons et ce que vous voulez. Nous sommes invités chez les gens pour y rencontrer la famille et les amis et cela nous honore. Vraiment.

~ Hildy Abrams, Presidente

A nosotros sí nos importa.

Todos los días nuestros clientes nos escriben cartas o nos envían correos electrónicos porque les encantan nuestros cubiertos. Estas cartas son muy importantes para nosotros porque se dirigen a lo que es nuestra pasión. Nos muestran que nos hemos puesto en contacto con lo que hacemos y con lo que Ud. quiere. Nos han invitado a algunos hogares a conocer a la familia y amigos y nos sentimos honrados. ¡De verdad!

~ Hildy Abrams, Presidente

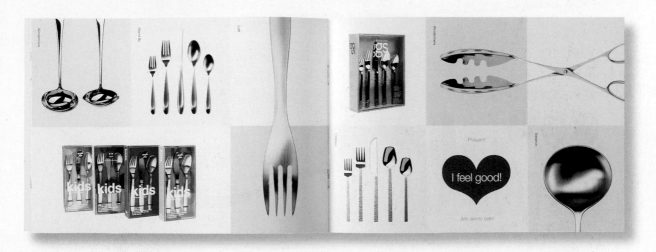

It's what Alison Hahn, a principal at the design firm, refers to as a trends-based approach to differentiation. After taking a hard look at silverware packaging, it became apparent that "conventions were rampant." This insight guided the team to work with Gourmet Settings to create a distinctive brand voice—one that extends from packaging to brochures. If you take your own retail tour, be sure to watch how consumers interact with the products on the shelf and snap a few pictures of the environment.

Smith warns, however, that small stores may not be happy about your snapping photos.

Anything you can do to become more familiar with a client's products or services will make the problem-solving process more effective. Hahn, for example, went for an eye exam and consultation when she worked on a brochure for a laser-eye surgery company. Though she couldn't see for a few hours after, it gave her firsthand knowledge of the client's

high standards for care and meticulous attention to detail. "Laser eye surgery is very competitive," she says. "We really needed to communicate the commitment and quality." Other information-gathering efforts are less time intensive. For example, the firm had the office administrator send a letter from home requesting a catalog from a client's competitor.

Visual freedom is possible.
What are you waiting for?

►▼ *As part of her research for this brochure, Alison Hahn, principal of Hahn Smith Design, visited the Herzig Eye Institute for a consultation and eye exam. "The free consultations are key to what they do," she says. Since many competitors' materials are cluttered, Hahn Smith worked with the client to hit key points and keep this piece simple.*

The Herzig Difference. At the Herzig Eye Institute our commitment is to provide each patient with their best possible vision correction, superior surgical treatments, and the highest level of patient care.

Medical Excellence. You have high expectations. We have the highest standards of medical excellence at the Herzig Eye Institute. Our team of renowned surgeons has been selected for their outstanding microsurgical experience in custom vision correction. Thanks to our superb track record, doctors across North America regularly and confidently refer their more difficult cases to us.

The Best Option for You. Your eyes are complex and precious. There is no one-size-fits-all solution. The Herzig Eye Institute specializes in precisely matching the appropriate treatment to a patient's unique needs to achieve their best possible vision. Your treatment may involve Laser Vision Correction or one of our other customized treatments. At the Herzig Eye Institute we utilize only the most advanced and proven vision correction technology to ensure we offer the best and safest option to you.

Excellence in Patient Care. We are committed to providing a full continuum of quality care from start to solution. From your thorough eye examination and personal consultation with your surgeon, to ensuring a comfortable and relaxed surgical procedure, to the very finest follow-up care during your recovery. Your care is our priority. We are also committed to keeping you fully informed. No question is too simple, no concern is too trivial. After all, the more you understand, the more confident you'll be in making the right decision. This unyielding passion for excellence in patient care is why the Herzig Eye Institute has been awarded the prestigious ISO 9001 certification.

The Herzig Lifetime Commitment. Our goal is 100% patient satisfaction. No gimmicks, and no surprises. Though infrequent, our surgeons will recommend a retreatment to further enhance your primary vision correction treatment if necessary, which of course we will do at no additional cost. At the Herzig Eye Institute our commitment is to provide you with your best possible vision. It's that simple.

www.herzig-eye.com

Our goal is 100% patient satisfaction. No gimmicks, and no surprises.

Be confident.
Imagine feeling assured about your appearance, and more importantly, being in control, less vulnerable to the annoying dependence on glasses and contacts. It's about being the best you can be. Why wait?

The Right Message

"Content is king," Hull says. Before his firm sits down to work out a design, they decide what they want to say. For a brochure for a rug dealer, for example, the firm met in the client's shop and listened to her stories about the background and origin of different rugs. Then the team came across a picture of Sigmund Freud's couch with a rug draped across it and discovered that the famous psychologist had written about rugs.

Stories seemed like the perfect way to help this client expand awareness about her business beyond the South. The resulting piece—Eight Rugs, Eight Stories—pairs gorgeous, original product shots with short literary excerpts about rugs. These hail from writers ranging from F. Scott Fitzgerald to Charles Dickens. First, the design team picked the stories, then the client helped pair each one with the most appropriate type of rug. They pulled it all together with a clean, classic feel.

In fact, it isn't uncommon to come up with the perfect concept after carefully listening to how your clients talk about their products. Hahn Smith, for example, based the concept for a Gourmet Settings brochure called "This is just a fork" on the way the company's president discussed the silverware. Designers sat in on sales meetings, met with suppliers, and heard the president talk about the products and company goals quite informally. This helped define the brochure's casual, friendly tone.

▼ *Though they sketched out the shots for this photo shoot in advance, Rigsby Hull made some changes based on the props available on-site. The shoot took place at a private home.*

eight rugs,
eight stories

a literary sampler
volume one

This is just a fork.

◀▼ *This brochure's content and tone was inspired by the way Gourmet Setting's president talks about her company and products. Hahn Smith used the piece to articulate the difference between this flatware company and its competitors.*

We know that. But we're obsessed. Forks (and knives and spoons) are what we're all about. Gourmet Settings really cares about flatware — in fact we're obsessed with it. This is our entire world.

It's just a fork — but it means everything to us.

It's personal. We'll replace it. We'll improve it. We'll find a new fork for the one you lost — even if it means that our president will go and find one for you. Personally.

We do a lot to earn your business — but we do even more to keep it.

Design Specifics

Page planning is another powerful tool in your brochure-design arsenal. Create a table of contents. Figure out the best way to unfold the story page by page. Think about pacing. Take a hard look at the text. "Don't tell the whole story on the cover," Hartford says. "Evolve the story over a series of pages."

As you decide what to include in a brochure, you may need to educate your client about the value of being concise. "They think of the printed page as real estate," Hartford says. "They want to build a high-rise when maybe they should be leaving a little bit of grass." Work with your client to edit down information to the essential points and talk with them about the value of making the piece more inviting to read. Focus on the most important information rather than trying to cram more on the page.

Sometimes, though, there's just no way to get around designing a text-heavy brochure—either because all that information is truly necessary, or the client insists on sticking with the extended copy. But this scenario doesn't mean a brochure has to be overwhelming for readers to navigate. Here are some ideas for making all that copy more manageable:

- Look for ways to break up the copy. Partner with the client or a copywriter to insert some catchy subheads where it's appropriate. Are there paragraphs that can be pulled out into sidebars or made into bullet points?

- Try varying the shape and size of the text block. It helps make the piece more approachable if there isn't the same square of copy staring out at readers from every page.

- Think about information architecture. Is it immediately clear what the most important message is on each page? And the second? As a rule of thumb, stick with no more than three levels of information on a given spread—a headline, deck, and body copy.

- Consider using pull quotes to break up blocks of copy. These can help draw readers into the text and make the amount of copy seem less intimidating.

- Mix things up with color. You might try making the body type, or perhaps just the subheads, a different shade. Sometimes even a colored paper can help brighten up a brochure with lots of text.

There are a lot of bases to cover before you start designing, but careful planning is the only way to make sure you're getting the right message across. As Hahn says, "It can be the most beautiful piece in the world, but if it doesn't communicate, it's a failure."

▲▶ Since this historic property is located on a canal, reflections became a theme for the piece. The concept is reinforced through the photography, which depicts actual reflections in the water as well as people reflecting in thought.

ORGANIZING AN INTERNATIONAL PHOTO SHOOT

It can seem like there are a hundred things to worry about before a photo shoot, but when you're coordinating one in another country, it becomes even more critical to pay attention to every detail. This was the situation facing Jason & Jason, a design firm based in Israel, after they were tapped to produce a high-end brochure to promote a commercial property in Amsterdam. Since the images needed to convey exclusivity, the design team decided to direct the shoot in person rather than rely on an unsupervised photographer. Jonathan Jason, executive creative director, walks us through the process he used to make the shoot successful—one that might work just as well for a photo session across town.

- **SCOUT THE LOCATION.** On Jason's first trip to Amsterdam, he checked out the building that would be featured in the brochure. "We use a simple pocket digital camera and shoot as many images as we can," he says.

- **SUBMIT SKETCHES TO THE CLIENT.** The design team uses the initial images to create sketches that show how the photo session will unfold. They try to include as many details as possible, such as how the models will be dressed, to keep the client informed.

- **HIRE AND BRIEF THE PHOTOGRAPHER.** Once the client approves the sketches, the firm locates a photographer and sends along the sketches. Then they discuss these ideas through email and phone conversations. On this shoot, the photographer was responsible for finding models, locating a stylist, arranging for props, and organizing the location.

- **BRING THE CLIENT TO THE SHOOT.** When possible, Jason recommends bringing a client representative to a shoot to authorize critical decisions. This makes it easy to get quick approval on a given shot. On this shoot, the client signed a waiver that gave creative authority to the design firm.

- **CHECK THE WEATHER FORECAST.** Since part of this photo shoot took place outside, the design team needed to build flexibility into their trip dates and the shoot schedule once they were in Amsterdam. "We had to cancel our trip plans twice because of weather," he says.

IDENTITY GUIDELINES ARE ONE OF THE ULTIMATE PLANNING TOOLS FOR GRAPHIC DESIGNERS. LIKE A WELL-WRITTEN BUSINESS PLAN, THEY PROVIDE A CONCRETE ROADMAP FOR THE FUTURE. THEY DEFINE WHAT A BRAND STANDS FOR AND HOW IT'S GOING TO BE PRESENTED VISUALLY—WHETHER YOU'RE WORKING ON A BUSINESS CARD OR A TEN-PAGE BROCHURE. THESE BRAND RULES MIGHT DEFINE EVERYTHING FROM CORRECT LOGO USAGE TO ACCEPTED COLOR PALETTES.

Working with Identity Guidelines

At Cincinnati Children's Hospital, a 43-page book helps make sure every project that passes through the hospital's marketing and communications department accurately reflects the brand. "These guidelines set the stage," says Andrea McCorkle, senior art director. "They're the foundation of any communication we do." The hospital's identity guidelines have evolved over time, but the current set emerged from a brand refresh.

During this rebranding process, the department conducted focus groups with different target audiences, including parents and referring physicians. This research helped refine the current visual identity. Parents, for instance, responded well to the hospital's bright, energetic color palette, but there was a need for something slightly more sophisticated when targeting doctors. This insight helped define the brand's secondary color palette, which features a wider range of choices.

The identity book also covers everything from how to use the logo on promotional items, such as T-shirts, hats, and mugs, to the hospital's photography style. Each section includes clear takeaway points for any designer working on the brand. Photos used for the hospital's materials, for example, should be editorial in style and shot with natural light when possible. In addition, the photography guidelines include benchmarks for composition, models, and model direction. This creates a cohesive look across a wide range of projects.

◄ *Cincinnati Children's Hospital identity guidelines come as part of a larger branding kit that includes editorial guidelines, paper samples, and a poster summarizing the brand. These materials keep the hospital's visual identity consistent across a range of materials created by both in-house and external designers.*

► *The target audience for this brochure was referring physicians nationwide, so it needed to have an added level of sophistication. To accomplish this, it uses colors from the brand's secondary palette, which is specifically designed to communicate sophistication and innovation.*

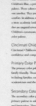

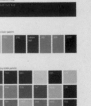

These rules and strategies pay off in countless ways, especially when it comes to maintaining the hospital's brand. "Our company is growing quickly, so more people are becoming heavier users of the brand who aren't in our department," McCorkle says. She uses the identity guidelines, for example, as a starting point when she out sources design work. It gives external graphic designers a crash course in the hospital's visual look and provides a great starting point to talk about specific projects.

All this upfront planning has also helped strengthen communication with the hospital's internal staff. "Sometimes a client will come in with a predetermined idea of what the piece will look like," she says. "We can use the ID guidelines to talk with them." In essence, the book provides an easy way to educate other departments about the hospital's brand. And though you might not find McCorkle flipping through the book at her computer—she knows the guidelines by heart—its content informs design decisions in all her work.

No matter how good the identity guidelines, there's still a lot of planning that needs to take place before you start working on a layout. McCorkle tends to kick off projects by meeting with the marketing representative—similar to an account

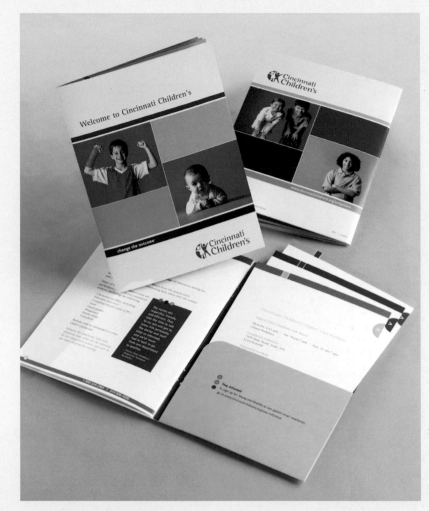

rep at an agency. They'll talk about the audience and the challenges at hand. She also makes sure to ask a lot of questions. For a piece about an outpatient MRI facility, she made sure to address differentiation: What makes us different from the competition? Why would someone choose this facility or service over other available options? What makes it better? Discussing these points helped her flesh out the creative aspects of the piece.

▲ This brochure kicks off with colorful grids on the front and back covers, a design element outlined in the hospital's branding guidelines. Every new patient at the hospital's outpatient locations receives this guide. It covers topics ranging from insurance to financial aid and provides information in an easily accessible format.

McCorkle recommends some of these same techniques for other designers, whether you're with an agency or working in-house. Start by asking a client whether they have guidelines and requesting samples of previous brochures and communications materials. Then prompt the company to identify the projects they considered successful and, if they're willing, ones they didn't think were up to par. Talking about these past efforts helps build a relationship and provides a framework as you move forward. Another good tactic: ask the client to identify a competitor who they feel may be marketing themselves better.

Once you've nailed all the hard questions, you can move back to those identity guidelines—assuming you're lucky enough to have them. They won't do the hard work for you, but they'll keep you on the same page as the rest of the brand.

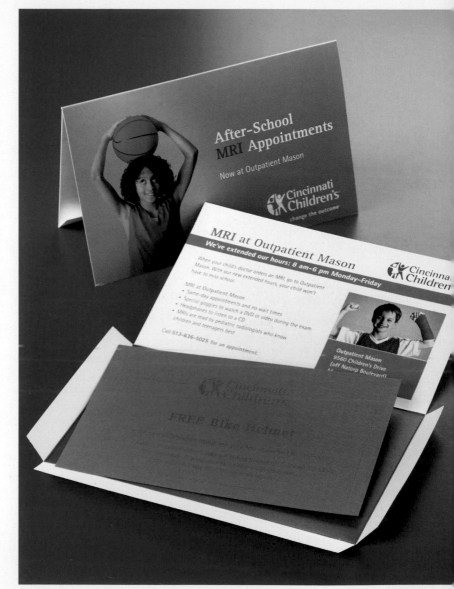

▲ *Like any good set of identity guidelines, Cincinnati Children's Hospital includes enough flexibility to encompass a range of projects and goals. This mailer, for example, is printed on a metallic paper to give it a special feel. There's a coupon for a free bike helmet inside, so designers wanted to differentiate it from other mailers.*

above & beyond

A PICTURE OF PROGRAMS THAT BENEFIT THE COMMUNITY

Cincinnati Children's
change the outcome®

◄▼ This brochure discusses how the hospital's programs benefit the community. The rounded corner on the photo caption represents a design element from the identity guidelines and helps pull attention to this spot on the spread.

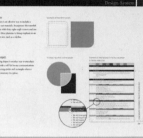

No Time to Wait
College Hill Campus Addresses a Critical Need

In 1995 the Emergency Department at Cincinnati Children's treated 800 children and adolescents with mental illness. In 2000 that number jumped to more than 2,000 – a 150 percent increase.

With cutbacks in state and federal funding and limited insurance reimbursement, families were forced to seek emergency solutions for chronic behavioral health illnesses or send their children out of the Tristate for longer-term, residential services. Where else could families turn?

Cincinnati Children's responded to this crisis by opening the College Hill Campus, a 60-bed psychiatric treatment center for children and adolescents requiring inpatient hospitalization for acute psychiatric care, residential treatment for chronic mental illness and outpatient psychiatric services.

Meeting the Need
"Before we opened the College Hill Campus, kids were leaving the area

and going to other states to get help for mental illness. We decided we needed to bring kids back," says Mike Sherlton, RN, senior clinical director of the Division of Child and Adolescent Psychiatry. "If we can treat them here, then as a community we can take care of our kids."

Paying the Price
From the beginning it was understood the cost to open and operate the College Hill Campus would be substantial. In fiscal year 2005 Cincinnati Children's lost more than $6 million on outpatient and residential mental health services at the medical center and the College Hill Campus. But the cost of not providing care to those suffering from conditions such as schizophrenia, bipolar disorder, major depressive disorder and obsessive-compulsive disorder would be far greater.

Without treatment those with mental illness face unnecessary disability, unemployment, substance abuse, homelessness, inappropriate incarceration and suicide. The National Alliance on Mental Illness estimates that the economic cost of untreated mental illness is more than $100 billion each year in the United States.

"We offer high-quality care to a population with desperate needs. The children we see often struggle with a major mental illness like bipolar disorder or severe depression, a history of abuse and neglect or exposure to violence, and cognitive impairment that challenges traditional methods of treatment," says Michael Sorter, MD, director of the Division of Child and Adolescent Psychiatry. Despite these realities, "Our outcomes demonstrate that mental health treatment works."

Family-Centered Care in Action
Having a child with mental illness can be difficult for all family members. Treatment plans take a multidisciplinary approach that includes family involvement. Parents and guardians are encouraged to visit their sons or daughters daily, take part in therapy sessions and talk with medical providers. Families learn about the roles of medication and therapy so treatment can continue successfully after a child leaves the campus. As their understanding of mental illness deepens, parents and guardians become equipped to manage their child's illness in ways that benefit the entire family.

Having a child with mental illness can be difficult for all family members. Treatment plans take a multidisciplinary approach that includes family involvement.

Measuring the Outcome
Since 2003, when residential treatment began at the College Hill Campus, more than 200 individuals have been through the program. Offering intensive treatment with an emphasis on family-centered care has significantly reduced the amount of time children are in treatment. The average length of stay for children in the residential program at the College Hill Campus is 90 days, compared to six months to a year in other residential treatment facilities across the country.

The treatment of mental illness comes in many forms. Recreational therapist Jill Fowee has teenagers from the College Hill Campus make weekly visits to a nearby nursing home to assist with activities, take walks and have conversations with the elderly residents.

"We give our kids a chance to do something for someone else," Jill says. "Making a difference in another person's life can improve physical and mental health, particularly for those who wrestle with depression and mental illness." ●

The College Hill Campus is a 60-bed psychiatric treatment center for children and adolescents requiring inpatient hospitalization for acute psychiatric care, residential treatment for chronic mental illness and outpatient psychiatric services.

Pet therapy is one of the recreational therapies at the College Hill Campus.

BY THE TIME THEY SOUGHT OUT A DESIGN FIRM, THE OUTFIT MEDIA GROUP ALREADY KNEW WHAT THEY WANTED: A LOGO AND A SIMPLE BROCHURE. THE HOLLYWOOD PRODUCTION COMPANY HAD RECENTLY BROKEN OFF FROM ANOTHER GROUP AND NEEDED TO PROMOTE ITS CAPABILITIES TO POTENTIAL CLIENTS. LUCKILY, THE COMPANY TURNED TO THE DECODER RING FOR HELP—AN AUSTIN-BASED DESIGN FIRM THAT ISN'T AFRAID TO ASK QUESTIONS.

Is a Brochure the Right Solution?

The design team took the time to understand the company's goals before they jumped into producing a brochure. What was Outfit Media Group trying to achieve? How is it different from the competition? It quickly became clear that a one-sheet—a simple brochure commonly used in this industry—wasn't going to grab attention. Designers also learned a key selling point for Outfit Media Group: the relatively small company could handle projects from start to finish.

This insight led to the idea for the logo, a one-eyed octopus with many legs. It represents a company with multiple capabilities (the legs) and a singular creative identity (the eye). Designers also decided a brochure wasn't the best way to promote Outfit Media to potential clients. "These one sheets either get thrown out or the best-case scenario is they get put into a file folder," says Christian Helms, a partner at The Decoder Ring. "We made it our goal to defy the file folder and the trash can."

The client liked the idea of a poster that recipients could hang on the wall, but designers decided to take things one step further and think of other ways this piece could work around the office. After a little brainstorming, they came up with a host of functional items to feature on the back of the poster, ranging from an air freshener and capabilities sheet to a DVD sleeve. These are things people might actually tear out and use, giving more promotional mileage to Outfit Media.

Think your clients would never go for such an offbeat solution? Try Helms' tips for working collaboratively and championing big ideas:

○ Think past the physical object. "Work harder and don't accept what you're told," Helms says. "Don't be a service bureau. If they say they want a logo, ask them why they want a logo. Ask what the goal is."

○ Listen and ask questions. Start with your initial contact, then move on to key decision-makers and even the secretary. "You never know where that insight is going to come from," Helms says. Rank and file employees often have a unique—and sometimes more realistic—perspective compared to their superiors.

○ Explain your process. "We show examples of other projects and talk about how they evolved," Helms says. You can't count on every client to know what designers do, so make the extra effort to illustrate your working methods and capabilities.

○ Work hard to build trust and strong relationships. "Come at these projects from the standpoint of being an advocate and a partner—not an authority," Helms says. "You don't ever want to talk down to your client." Nor should you approach a client as an adversary.

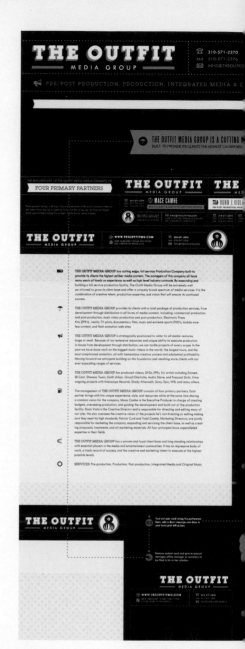

▲ Though the client originally wanted a brochure, The Decoder Ring worked with them to uncover a better solution—this 18 x 24–inch (45.7 x 61–cm) poster. It gave the Hollywood production company more face time with potential clients and turned into a conversation piece in many offices. People passing through asked who the Outfit Media Group was and what they did. The back features a host of items for people to tear out and use, ranging from an air freshener to a capabilities sheet.

BASICS

"YOU NEED TO APPEAL TO PEOPLE WHO ONLY HAVE 15 SECONDS TO DETERMINE IF THEY HAVE MORE TIME TO SPEND WITH THE PIECE." —KENN FINE, FOUNDER AND CREATIVE DIRECTOR AT FINE DESIGN GROUP

A GREAT BROCHURE NEEDS BEAUTY AND BRAINS. SURE, IT NEEDS TO LOOK GOOD, BUT IT ALSO NEEDS TO EFFECTIVELY DELIVER A MESSAGE–TYPICALLY MORE THAN ONE. WHETHER IT'S MEANT TO SELL CONDOS OR RAISE MONEY FOR A NONPROFIT, A SUCCESSFUL BROCHURE SHOULD DRAW READERS IN WITH A SMART LAYOUT TO ACHIEVE A LARGER GOAL.

Layout: Spinning a Yarn

"It's really a storytelling challenge," says Tamara Dowd, a creative director at Hirshorn Zuckerman Design Group (HZDG) in Rockville, Maryland. "How does it unfold?" The best designers lay out a brochure with the same care a fiction writer takes when plotting a short story.

Unlike a postcard or print ad, these multipage pieces require a narrative to pull people along. Great brochures deliver compelling messages in just the right order. Like an engrossing novel, they keep readers turning the pages. A brochure might pose a question on the first spread or two then provide the answer later in the piece. Another approach? Lead with the sexiest message and then present more in-depth information once the target audience is hooked. "I think, in general, a lot of people don't think about flow," says Andrew Wicklund, a design director at Hornall Anderson Design Works in Seattle. "They don't see the big picture."

A multipage print piece should build suspense or interest, and there needs to be a natural progression from spread to spread. If there's too much redundancy, readers are likely to lose interest, but a layout that changes radically with every page flip doesn't work, either. A winning project must master this and countless other balancing acts. "With a brochure, there's a lot of interplay between words and images," says Travis Cain, a senior designer at Planet Propaganda in Madison, Wisconsin "They're constantly being put together." A successful layout needs to integrate these two elements in service of the larger message.

▲ *"If it's long-form like this, you have to think in terms of the story as opposed to the design at first," says Andrew Wicklund, a design director at Hornall Anderson Design Works in Seattle. "Put the bones in. Develop the structure and hierarchy and then start to develop aesthetic." This promotional piece for an upcoming commercial building, for instance, revolves around three key selling points: professionalism, productivity, and proximity.*

The Director's Chair

Dowd believes that planning out how a brochure's story will unfold is a bit like directing a movie. After all, you're in control of the images, order and pacing—and you probably hold some sway over the copy, too. She's a big advocate of taking the time to rough out a storyboard before moving to the computer. This process gives you the chance to think about pacing and creates a structured outline of all the elements that a particular brochure requires. You won't find yourself missing a crucial image or message halfway through the final layout.

So grab a stack of 3 x 5–inch (7.6 x 12.7–cm) cards—they make it easy to play with order—or draw squares on a sheet of paper to represent each spread. Then start making simple notes about what goes where. At HZDG, for example, Dowd and the design team often tackle real estate brochures, which present a special set of challenges. How do you make people fall in love with a building that isn't built yet? You create a piece with personality, emotion, and a strong concept. The design team at HZDG, for instance, might debate whether to tell the story of the community or building first. Which one is the better hook? Or they might flag a particularly striking image to run across the center spread. Once there's a rough map, they ask another critical question. "This all makes sense, but what part of the story aren't we telling?" Dowd says.

There's also something to be said for making your first layout on the computer a rough one. Cain likes to place the images and copy all the way through—even if he's using placeholders for some elements. This gives him a good idea of the ratio of text to artwork and allows him to figure out where everything needs to go. "A rough layout allows you to start thinking spread to spread how these images and copy are going to come together," he says. From there, he works to refine the design and fill in sections with the actual art and copy, as they're available. Sometimes he needs to make adjustments once those final elements are in place. "It's a fluid process," he says. "You need to be flexible."

► *To maneuver readers through this Jobster brochure, the design team at Hornall Anderson Design Works in Seattle varied the scale of the imagery—and the way the type is treated—from spread to spread. This piece represents part of a larger rebranding project for the online recruitment and career-networking site.*

Too Busy to Read

In an ideal world, your target audience would spend half an hour pouring over every detail of your brochure. In reality, however, they're more likely to spend a few seconds making a snap decision as they sort mail over the trash can. Or if you're really lucky, you'll garner a minute or two as they wait for a delayed flight at the airport. "What's the chance of getting them to sit down and focus on it with a glass of wine?" says Kenn Fine, founder and creative director at FINE Design Group in San Francisco. "You need to appeal to people who only have 15 seconds to determine if they have more time to spend with the piece."

What is his antidote to this time crunch? Figure out the most important thing a brochure needs to say and make sure that message comes across in five seconds. Then identify the second and third most crucial points and think about them as the 30-second experience. Since what a piece says is just as important as how it looks, you'll want to consider the experience of reading a brochure as you're designing it. What comes

◄ *This brochure's pages—printed on heavy stock—are held together with a rubber band at the top of the piece. "We're always trying to find a way to differentiate," says Jennifer Higgins, a senior art director at HZDG. "The condominium market is oversaturated."*

across after glancing at the cover? Or after flipping through the first few spreads? Is the message easy to digest in the middle of a hectic day? Do the key points stand out first?

It might also help to adopt Dowd's approach and think about three different levels of reading: main headlines and pictures; main headlines, pictures, and sidebars; or the full piece. Take a few minutes to consider what readers would take away from each of these experiences. Does the core message come across in the display copy and images? Or is it buried in the body copy? "You need to communicate the basic sell without the full read," Dowd says. "You can't guarantee that someone's going to give you that much time in their life to read an entire brochure."

▼ *Seattle-based design firm Hornall Anderson Design Works created this brochure as the first piece of collateral for Eos Airlines. "We were pretty generous with the amount of space we allowed for each idea or topic," says design director Mark Popich. "The type is fairly quiet. We wanted to create a calming, refined aesthetic." This type of approach matches the upscale feel the design team created for the whole piece, with such thoughtful details as iridescent paper.*

Vying for Attention

With to-do lists growing like weeds, sometimes it takes a slightly different approach to get someone to pick up a brochure at all. "We really push hard on formats," says Dowd, about her work at HZDG. The firm does a lot of pieces to promote upcoming condos—a competitive market in the D.C. area. One way they help clients stand out is with format ideas that are original but still appropriate.

A brochure for a mixed-use development called Rockville Town Square, for example, comes in an interesting package. "Early on we thought, 'This needs to be in a shopping bag,'" she says. "It's a live, work, shop, play concept. We really wanted to call attention to the fact that you're going to be living above everything you'll ever need." The piece comes inside an elegant brown shopping bag with ribbon handles—one that fits right in with the bags used by high-end retailers. For another development, the firm created a cover for a brochure that slides off to reveal a friendly neighborhood map. "I had a professor in college who would call it 'the kiss,'" Dowd says. "It's one little thing beyond what's expected, and it's always in service of the product."

When considering alternate formats, however, it's key to think about what the audience is used to getting and how they're going to use the piece. For example, Wicklund worked on a brochure for an upcoming commercial development in Seattle, and he originally wanted to significantly break from the 8½ x 11–inch (20.3 x 27.9–cm) format used by most of the building's competitors. After talking with the client, however, he discovered that this conservative audience was comfortable with this standard size—in part because it fits easily in file folders and binders—so he went with a 7½ x 11–inch (17.8 x 27.9–cm) piece. This information also led to another functional design detail: Wicklund chose looped staples so the piece would easily slip onto a three-ring binder.

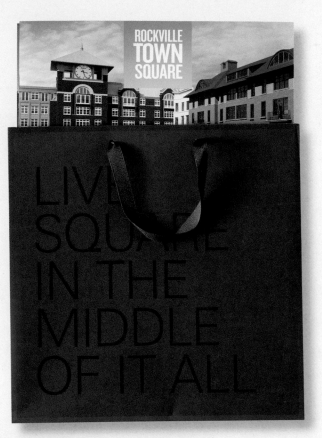

◀▼ *Instead of a ho-hum product folder, designers at HZDG put this brochure in a shopping bag to grab attention. This choice also reinforces the development's "Live, Work, Shop, Play" concept. Along with a migrating varnish, the bag gives the piece an upscale feel.*

LIVE. WORK. SHOP. PLAY.

The four sides of your life that make a perfect Square: **Rockville Town Square**, the new downtown Rockville. Five buildings of luxury condominiums directly above street-level retail. It's a whole new way of life. A place where everything you need is moments away, not miles. Where commuting means you're just **two blocks from Metro**. Where your favorite shops and restaurants are your neighbors. And the centerpiece is a **vibrant town square**—a gathering place bigger than a football field for farmers' markets, concerts, community celebrations, and **simply enjoying life**, every day.

ONCE YOU'VE GOT THE BIG-PICTURE DECISIONS DOWN, THERE ARE STILL THE SMALL-SCALE ONES TO IRON OUT. IT'S A BIT LIKE CHOOSING EXACTLY THE RIGHT PROPS ON A MOVIE SET. IS THAT LAMP WORKING? OR SHOULD IT BE A LITTLE SMALLER? "IT'S VERY IMPORTANT THAT DESIGNERS REALIZE THAT, TO TAKE A PIECE TO ANOTHER LEVEL, THEY HAVE TO BE WILLING TO DO THE NITTY GRITTY," SAYS JEFFERSON LIU, A SENIOR ART DIRECTOR AT HZDG.

Finishing Touches

When he worked on a promotional piece for a condo development called View14, he rolled up his sleeves and made sure the smallest details were just right. The brochure features a series of interior renderings, but to make them more engaging, Liu and the interior designer teamed up to decorate these virtual rooms. They searched for real pieces of furniture that sent the message they were trying to convey and worked together to arrange them in the spaces. All these details were sent to the rendering company, so they could make each virtual room come to life. As a result, the condos in this yet-to-be-built development seem tangible. You can imagine living there, because the design shows you how the condos might look once you add your own style.

As details evolve, it's also essential to approach the design process organically. On View14, for example, everyone from the architects to the developers was just as detail-oriented as the graphic-design team. These collaborators might request that a sink or cabinet be moved an inch or two within a particular rendering—small adjustments that more accurately reflect the final product. "I think it's important in design not to be married to anything," Liu says. "Beginning designers, once they get things perfect, are afraid to change it." Fine suggests another important strategy: if time permits, step away from the design for a day or two and come back to it with fresh eyes. It's an easy way to check your own work.

◄▼ These renderings show what it might be like to live in these future condos. Liu worked with the interior designer to pick out furniture and arrange the pieces within the spaces. These details were forwarded to the rendering company.

► *"Our mission here was to create an almost anti–real estate brochure," says Jefferson Liu, a senior art director at HZDG. "No shiny happy people." Instead of showing a generic couple or someone jogging in the park, this piece focuses on the condo development's style. Small details—like the fish swimming down this spread—help set the piece apart. A koi pond planned for the building's lobby inspired this addition.*

COMMITTING TO THE DETAILS

If this elegant fundraising brochure somehow morphed into a mystery novel, its title just might be *The Hunt for Blue Matches*. Hornall Anderson Design Works designed this piece—largely as a pro bono effort—to help aishSeattle solicit funds from prominent donors. The Jewish educational and outreach organization needed something to leave behind when calling on potential supporters.

The Z-fold brochure features two covers and, in essence, two different stories. One side reveals the organization's emotional and spiritual side, following a little girl as she celebrates with her family. "It needed to touch the heart," says Yuri Shvets, a graphic designer at the Seattle firm. "It could not look like a capabilities book." The piece's flip side focuses more on the businesslike details, explaining aishSeattle's programs, goals, and budget.

But for designers, there's a bigger message: don't give up on the details. Shvets wanted to include an actual match on one of the covers, but its tip needed to be the same shade as the blue candle on the other cover. "I was researching all the matches in the world," Shvets says. "The vendors had every color in the rainbow but that exact hue." Finally, he found a company that could reproduce the color, but the custom mix was simply too expensive for this low-budget project.

The vendor, however, sent 50 matches as a sample, which meant Shvets only needed to locate 200 more for this tiny print run. As luck would have it, one weekend, he stumbled upon the solution. He was eating at a restaurant whose matchbooks contained the perfect shade of blue. Shvets pocketed a sufficient quantity for his project—hardly more than any other patron might pick up. "We got lucky," he adds.

So why not take the faster route and create a 3D effect in Photoshop? Shvets wanted the additional value offered by a tactile object—a choice that makes the brochure seem less manufactured and more tailored. "We strive for the highest standards," he says. "Even for pro bono pieces." Additionally, aishSeattle made the commitment to place all those matches in the tiny envelopes and glue them on each cover by hand. Shvets even took the time to write up instructions for the process. After all, it's the details that light the fire.

▼ *The design team at Hornall Anderson Design Works in Seattle felt strongly about including an actual 3D match on the cover of this fundraising brochure, but finding matches in the right shade of blue—and at the right price—was harder than they imagined.*

EIGHT TACTICS FOR SMARTER TYPOGRAPHY

··· **READ THE COPY.** When you're on deadline, it's tempting to skim the text rather than take the time to give it a thorough read. But really understanding what's being communicated in all that gray gives you the knowledge to present the copy in the best way for readers. You might come up with ideas for making the copy more accessible—with headlines, subheads, and sidebars—and you'll definitely have a better handle on the overall message.

··· **LESS IS MORE.** There are countless typefaces to choose from for any given project, but your best bet is often restraint. Thinking about using more than two fonts? Take a few minutes to consider whether those extra typefaces are really enhancing the project. Put yourself in the reader's shoes and reflect on the piece's overall readability.

··· **LEARN THE HISTORY.** The right typeface should enhance your project's concept rather than fight against it. But in order to know what message you're sending, you need to familiarize yourself with a font's history. Is it 10 years old? 20? Or older? What was the intention when it was created? These answers should tell you whether a typeface works for that brochure or whether it's time to look at other options.

··· **SWEAT THE SMALL STUFF.** Much of good typography lies in the details. Pay attention to letter spacing—especially between upper and lowercase letters—and be on the lookout for widows and orphans. Also take a close look at the rag to make sure it isn't inadvertently attracting a viewer's attention by forming odd shapes.

··· **EMBRACE HIERARCHY.** Sure, there's a movement toward less hierarchy at many businesses. But when it comes to type, these differing levels of importance make copy easier to read and understand—not to mention less intimidating. Everything from headlines to pull quotes gives people a hand organizing and remembering information. A good rule of thumb: there shouldn't be more than three levels of importance within a single layout.

··· **CONQUER TEXT OVERPOPULATION.** Too much text—coupled with too little art and space—creates another problem entirely. If you're dealing with reams of text, try going back to the client and working with them to hone the message. Also look for ways to use some of the text as artwork, either with pull quotes or attractive sidebars. It can also help to experiment with the color of the type and the space between paragraphs. Focus on ways to break up those heavy text blocks so you're not creating the same shape on every page.

··· **EXPLORE YOUR OPTIONS.** Rather than rely on a handful of tried and true typefaces, make an effort to keep up on the latest offerings in the type world. Not every project calls for a trendy new font, but it's good to know what's available. Other ideas: Try using an ampersand instead of the word "and" in display copy. Or experiment with old-style numbers; since they don't sit on the baseline like more typical numbers, they blend in better with body copy.

··· **COLLECT TYPE.** Feel like your approach to type is getting stale? Restock those creative stores by starting a type collection. Whether it's the placemat at the Chinese restaurant or a quick snapshot of a poster on the street, make a point to collect things that catch your eye and store them away for those rainy days when your inspiration is flagging.

SIZE MATTERS

For once, spammers might be onto something: bigger can be better. When the group putting together New York City's Olympic bid hired Giampietro+Smith to design a brochure, they wanted the firm to create a piece that tugged at the heart strings of Olympic delegates. The brochure was slated to land on desks about two weeks after an 800-page bid book—a document that made the logistical case for New York's Olympic dreams, but not necessarily the emotional one.

To solve this problem, designers sat down with a copywriter and created a series of compelling headlines based on concepts outlined in the Olympic Charter. Phrases like "People will speak your language" and "There's room for everyone" evoked both the Olympic spirit and New York's multicultural landscape. But the firm still needed to figure out the best way to present these short and spare sentiments. "How do you get someone to stop and pay attention when there are only a few words?" says Rob Giampietro, a principal at the New York firm. "We made it the size of a billboard."

The piece showed up at offices in a rigid 19 x 23-inch (22.9 x 58.4 cm) envelope, a size that's hard to ignore no matter how long your to-do list. Printed on a white newspaper sheet, the piece intersperses copy with

sports action shots and vivid New York scenes. The oversized sheets are folded in half and fit together just like the morning newspaper. (Stapling would have caused the large sheets to rip.) Though New York ultimately lost its Olympic bid, the piece was well-received by delegates, and New York's bid committee liked the brochure's headlines so much that they used them for an outdoor advertising campaign around the city.

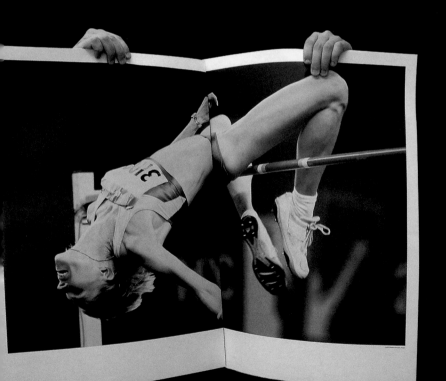

people will speak your language

There are no foreigners in New York City. Our citizens come from every country. Every language is spoken. Every holiday is celebrated. Every spirit is worshipped. Every tradition is shared. Every spice is available. Every nation is represented and every flag is raised.

Since its founding, New York has been home to a multi-national, multi-racial, multi-religious, and multi-cultural community. Our of the 201 Olympic nations that competed in Athens, 198 have children enrolled in the New York City public schools. At a 2012 Olympic Games in New York, there will be no language or cultural barriers. Our families will welcome your families and new friends will be your guides.

▲◄ *Since it was mailed to a highly sought-after audience—the delegates who pick future Olympic cities—this brochure needed to command attention. "At some point, we had the idea of, 'Let's make it the size of their desks so it doesn't get lost on their desks,'" says Rob Giampietro, a principal at New York firm Giampietro+Smith.*

Fifty Inspiring Ideas

Do you have so many deadlines that you're starting to feel like a hamster running on a wheel? Try a few of these ideas to keep the needle on your creative gauge pointing toward full.

1. **TAKE A FORTY-EIGHT-HOUR COMPUTER VACATION.**
   No email. No Google. No one last peek at that brochure you need to present to the client on Monday morning.

2. **TRY MEDITATION.**
   Filmmaker David Lynch swears his daily practice is crucial to all his creative work.

3. **LEARN SOMETHING NEW THAT ISN'T DIRECTLY RELATED TO YOUR JOB.**
   Sign up for a fencing class or master the art of baking puff pastries.

4. **FIND A MENTOR—THEY'RE NOT JUST FOR STUDENTS.**
   Look for someone whose work you admire or who simply excels in a single area where you'd like to expand your skills.

5. **CHANGE THE SCENERY.**
   When you feel stuck, pack up your laptop and head to the park or the corner coffee shop. An environmental shift might be enough to shake things loose.

6. **FORM A SKETCHING HABIT.**
   Buy a small notebook and tuck it in your bag. Then use life's spare moments—standing in line at the DMV or sitting in gridlock traffic— to draw what's around you.

7. **SET A THIRTY-DAY CREATIVE CHALLENGE FOR YOURSELF.**
   Maybe it's coming up with four concepts for every project that crosses your desk this month instead of three. Or temporarily giving up your blog habit and spending the found time designing a poster a week.

8. **PRETEND YOU'RE NOT A GRAPHIC DESIGNER.**
   How would a carpenter handle a difficult client? What would a lawyer do if he or she were snowed under with deadlines? Look for approaches and best practices to adopt from other business arenas.

9. **FIND A GOAL BUDDY.**
Check in with each other once a week about your creative aspirations and how you're going to achieve them. It adds accountability when those personal goals start slipping to the bottom of your to-do list.

10. **PLAY BEAT THE CLOCK.**
Is your motivation flagging at 3:00 P.M.? Set an egg timer for thirty or sixty minutes and challenge yourself to get as much done as possible. You can always revise this fast-paced work later.

11. **SEARCH OUT OLD BOOKS AND MAGAZINES AT ANTIQUE OR JUNK SHOPS.**
Those ads and layouts might shake loose some fresh ideas.

12. **DITCH THE MUSEUM AND SPEND SOME TIME APPRECIATING CHILDREN'S ARTWORK.**
The paintings hanging on the wall at your niece's grade school might offer more imaginative ideas than revisiting the Old Masters.

13. **KEEP A FOUND OBJECT COLLECTION.**
Stuff anything that catches your eye—from the type on a takeout menu to the hierarchy on a piece of junk mail—into a box or file drawer. Then pull them back out when you're in brainstorming mode.

14. **BRUSH UP ON PAPER AND PRINTING TECHNIQUES.**
When the right project arises, these can become innovative tools for communicating a concept.

15. **GO ON A FACT-FINDING MISSION.**
Working on a brochure for an unfamiliar industry? Take the time to read up on widget-making or mortgage insurance. You might stumble on some context or history that illuminates the problem at hand.

16. **REVIEW PAST PROJECTS FOR THE SAME CLIENT.**
Did you miss any opportunities to articulate the message? Can those be rolled forward into this piece?

17. **STOP BEING SO SERIOUS.**
Take fifteen minutes and intentionally come up with ridiculous concepts for the project sitting on your desk. You might stumble on something useful. You'll definitely relieve some pressure.

18. GET UP AND MOVE AROUND.

Spend ten minutes away from the computer screen. Walk around the block, dust off your bookshelves, or go make silly faces at the account reps. A little physical activity might give your subconscious a chance to brew up some creative solutions.

19. ASK FOR ADVICE.

Whether you describe your problem to your cube neighbor or your mom, you're likely to get a fresh perspective. Just putting the creative dilemma into words might give rise to a few ideas.

20. DRAW SOMETHING FIFTY TIMES.

Pick any object—from the stapler on your desk to your cat—and draw it fifty times. No fair giving up halfway through. You'll force yourself to look past the obvious and stretch your idea-generating capacity.

21. BOARD GAMES ANYONE?

Stash board games at the office and break them out on slow days or when the brain drain hits on Friday afternoon. An hour of fun promotes bonding and helps put you back in touch with your sense of wonder.

22. GO SHOPPING!

Grab a fellow designer and go on a retail tour. Look for stores you don't normally shop at and take a close look at everything from hang tags and packaging to environmental graphics. Who do you think frequents this store? Do these people overlap with the target market for any of the projects sitting on your desk?

23. WORD EXERCISES.

Write 100 words about the project you're working on as fast as humanly possible. Look back at these unedited thoughts and see whether there's a key point to pull out and build on.

24. EXPERIMENT WITH DIFFERENT SOFTWARE.

Always work in Illustrator? Pop open InDesign for your next brochure. Want a real challenge? See how much fancy footwork you can do with a nondesign program like Microsoft Word.

25. BUY NEW SCHOOL SUPPLIES.

Remember what a rush it was to pick out a new Trapper Keeper? Update your desk with some fun new basics. Spring for the fancy pens or pretty magazine holders and give serious consideration to a 64-pack of Crayola crayons.

26. FIGURE OUT YOUR CREATIVE CRUTCHES; THEN THROW THEM OUT.
Falling back on a favorite font a little too often? Using a similar shape or effect in one too many layouts? Make a list of banned items and stick with it for thirty days.

27. PRETEND THAT EVERY CLIENT IS YOUR FAVORITE.
You're more likely to go the extra mile—and less likely to get irritated at suggestions.

28. REARRANGE YOUR OFFICE.
Or if that's not possible, simply reorganize the things on and in your desk. A slight change in environment can give you a creative boost.

29. WRITE YOUR DREAM PROFESSIONAL BIO.
Then work backward to see what you need to do right now to put yourself on the path to making it come true.

30. WRITE A LETTER TO YOUR CREATIVE HERO—LIVING OR DEAD.
In the letter, outline what you find so inspiring about his or her work. You might just get back in touch with what made you so excited about design in the first place.

31. PULL OUT YOUR SENIOR PORTFOLIO FROM COLLEGE.
Seeing where you started—and how far you've come—can be a powerful experience.

32. MAKE A CHANGE IN YOUR DAILY ROUTINE.
Leave the car at home next week while you take the bus or eat lunch at a hole-in-the-wall diner instead of at your desk. Breaking up your routine may introduce new influences into your life.

33. LOG OFF THE INTERNET AND HEAD FOR THE BRICKS-AND-MORTAR LIBRARY.
Peruse the stacks and flip through the books at random. Find a comfy chair and split your time between reading and observing your fellow patrons.

34. TAKE ON A FREELANCE PROJECT THAT'S COMPLETELY DIFFERENT FROM YOUR REGULAR WORK.
You'll likely bring fresh ideas back to your day job.

35. LOOK FOR INSPIRATION IN THE LEAST LIKELY PLACES.
Working on a project for men? Flip through a women's magazine or catalog to check out designs meant for the opposite sex.

36. START AN INFORMAL CRITIQUE GROUP.
Get together once a month with other creative thinkers—everyone from painters and writers to designers—to share and discuss favorite work from each person in the group.

37. CONSIDER BRINGING HANDMADE ELEMENTS INTO YOUR WORK.
What about burning or distressing paper? Can you draw the illustration yourself? What about building small props for a photo shoot?

38. MAKE CREATIVITY A HABIT.
Even when you're sitting in meetings all day, try to carve out at least an hour to touch base with a hands-on creative task—whether that's working on a rough layout or doing a sketch for your own enjoyment.

39. KEEP RANDOM LISTS.
Jot down people you admire, books you'd like to read, tech toys you want to buy, places to visit before you die, unbelievable facts—anything that captures your fancy.

40. PICK TWO PEOPLE, COUNTRIES, OR BRANDS THAT SEEM LIKE POLAR OPPOSITES.
Then spend fifteen minutes listing as many similarities between them as you can.

41. QUESTION YOUR ASSUMPTIONS.
Does this brochure have to be the same size as the last one? Is the target audience exactly the same? Is there wiggle room in the budget? Can you use illustrations instead of photos?

42. LOOK FOR INSPIRATION IN THE EVERYDAY OBJECTS AROUND YOU.

Take another look at the pencil cup on your desk. Empty it out. Turn it upside down. Look inside. Challenge yourself to discover something new about one of these humdrum items.

43. HIRE A CREATIVITY COACH.
Even if you're not in a rut, they can help you clarify your goals and push you to the next level.

44. TEACH A CLASS.
Even if it's not related to design, you'll practice explaining concepts in a way that's clear and inviting—a skill to brush up on for client.

45. KEEP YOUR OWN PERSONAL RALLY GEAR AT YOUR DESK.
When your side of the scoreboard seems to be slipping, put on a ball cap, novelty glasses, or even a pirate's eyepatch to shake things up.

46. FEELING LUCKY?
Enter a few key words related to your project into the Google search box and hit the "I'm feeling lucky" button.

47. START OVER.
Throw away your best idea and make yourself start the brainstorming process over. You might be surprised at what else you come up with.

48. DON'T LOOK AT THE CLOCK.
Stop paying attention to how much time it's taking you to come up with an idea or work out some rough spots in a design. Cover up the clocks and focus on the work—ignoring those deadline constraints for a bit.

49. FLIP OPEN A NOVEL IN THE MIDDLE AND READ ONLY THOSE TWO PAGES.
Then guess the main plot of the book and make predictions about what's going to happen to those characters. What kind of clothes do they wear? Where do they live? What kind of furniture do they have? Give your invention skills a workout.

50. USE SOMETHING FOR A PURPOSE OTHER THAN WHAT WAS INTENDED.
Draw pictures on your white tennis shoes. Create letters with chopsticks or paper clips.

BUDGET
CONSIDE

RATIONS

"I NEVER LET SMALL BUDGETS HINDER MY CREATIVITY. THE CHALLENGE OF GRAPHIC DESIGN FOR ME IS PROBLEM SOLVING." —NOAH SCALIN, FOUNDER OF ANOTHER LIMITED REBELLION

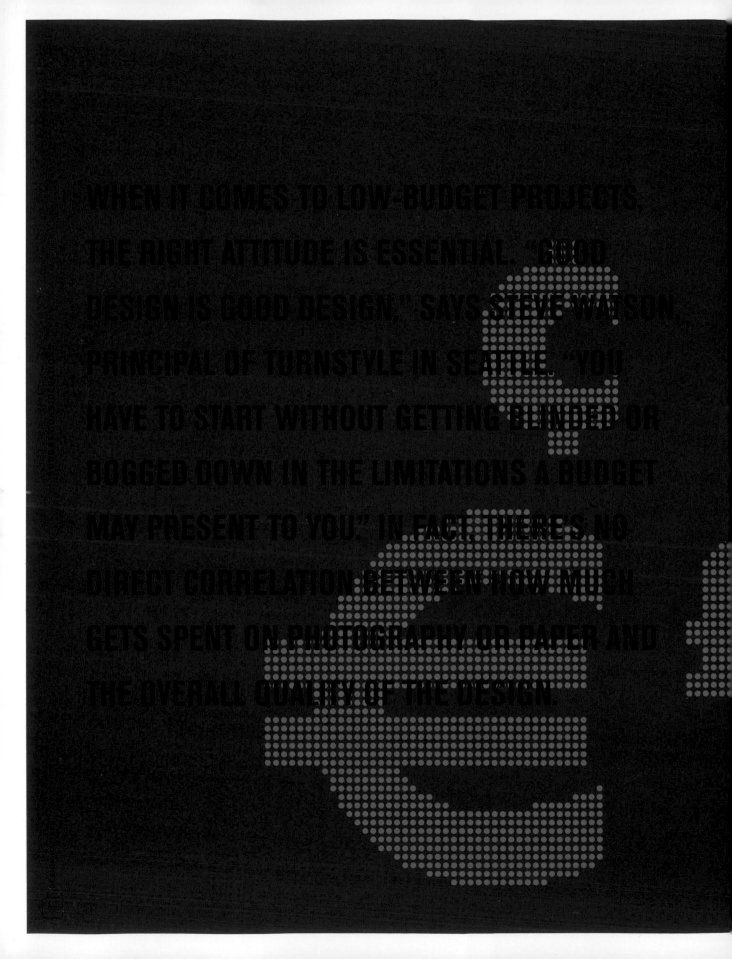

WHEN IT COMES TO LOW-BUDGET PROJECTS, THE RIGHT ATTITUDE IS ESSENTIAL. "GOOD DESIGN IS GOOD DESIGN," SAYS STEVE WATSON, PRINCIPAL OF TURNSTYLE IN SEATTLE. "YOU HAVE TO START WITHOUT GETTING BLINDED OR BOGGED DOWN IN THE LIMITATIONS A BUDGET MAY PRESENT TO YOU." IN FACT, THERE'S NO DIRECT CORRELATION BETWEEN HOW MUCH GETS SPENT ON PHOTOGRAPHY OR PAPER AND THE OVERALL QUALITY OF THE DESIGN.

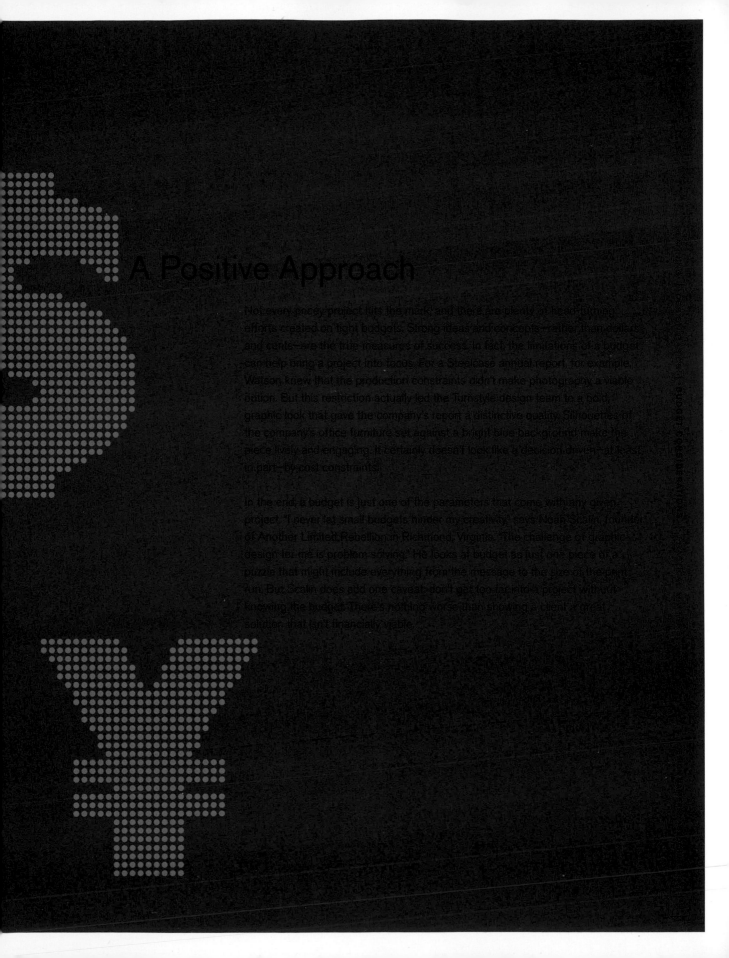

A Positive Approach

Not every pricey project hits the mark, and there are plenty of head-turning efforts created on tight budgets. Strong ideas and concepts—rather than dollars and cents—are the true measures of success. In fact, the limitations of a budget can help bring a project into focus. For a Steelcase annual report, for example, Watson knew that the production constraints didn't make photography a viable option. But this restriction actually led the Turnstyle design team to a bold, graphic look that gave the company's report a distinctive quality. Silhouettes of the company's office furniture set against a bright blue background make the piece lively and engaging. It certainly doesn't look like a decision driven—at least in part—by cost constraints.

In the end, a budget is just one of the parameters that come with any given project. "I never let small budgets hinder my creativity," says Noah Scalin, founder of Another Limited Rebellion in Richmond, Virginia. "The challenge of graphic design for me is problem solving." He looks at budget as just one piece of a puzzle that might include everything from the message to the size of the print run. But Scalin does add one caveat: don't get too far into a project without knowing the budget. There's nothing worse than showing a client a great solution that isn't financially viable.

◄ *Despite being printed on fairly modest paper at a financial printer, this Steelcase annual report creates an engaging narrative. The flood of color on this cover, for instance, immediately grabs attention.*

► *This text-heavy spread stays approachable with bold typography and color. The pull quote breaks up the running text, while changes in type color make the extensive copy less intimidating to read.*

► *Since photography wasn't a viable option with this project's production constraints, the designers at Turnstyle created silhouettes of Steelcase's products. "Their furniture creates very iconic shapes," says principal Steve Watson.*

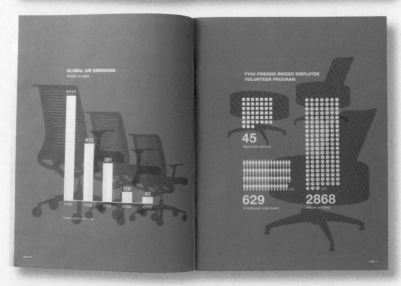

▲ *Noah Scalin, founder of Another Limited Rebellion, stretched a small budget by designing something with more than one function. This brochure—promoting a summer theater program—becomes a poster when unfolded. It's twice the marketing punch with a single printed piece.*

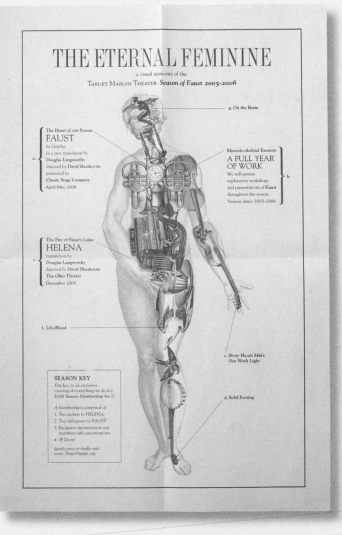

▲▶ *This unassuming mailer folds out into a striking poster. The strength of the concept—a woman depicted through an image collage—makes an impact without high production costs. Noah Scalin, founder of Another Limited Rebellion, also saved money by creating the collage himself from stock illustrations.*

KNOWING YOUR WAY AROUND THE PRODUCTION END OF A PROJECT IS A BIT LIKE FINDING A HUNDRED DOLLAR BILL ON THE SIDEWALK. WHEN THERE'S A TIGHT BUDGET, IT'S KEY TO THINK THROUGH HOW A PIECE WILL BE PRODUCED BEFORE YOU START DESIGNING. A SMALL CHANGE IN TRIM SIZE OR PAPER CAN MAKE OR BREAK YOUR BUDGET.

Production Strategies

Noah Scalin, founder of ALR Design, sometimes heads straight to the printer with his budget and print-run requirements, then he asks for advice about what is possible. A small change in the size of a brochure, for instance, might make it fit better on the press sheet and significantly reduce costs. Unfortunately, there's no magic formula to spitting out the most cost-effective print strategy for every job. One- or two-color printing, for instance, doesn't necessarily save money over four-color. The cost of any print job depends on variables ranging from the size of the print run to who provided the bid. But there are some general strategies to help stretch those production dollars. Justin Ahrens, creative director of Rule29 in Geneva, Illinois, offers these tips:

- BUILD STRONG RELATIONSHIPS WITH YOUR VENDORS. If you throw a lot of business to a particular photographer or printer, they're going to be more willing to work with you when you're trying to meet tight parameters.

- TALK TO YOUR PAPER REP ABOUT WHAT CHOICES ARE AVAILABLE. If you have a specific stock in mind, he or she might be able to point you to something similar with a lower price tag.

- ASK YOUR PRINTER ABOUT THE HOUSE SHEET. Typically, this is a paper purchased at a discount and may be a way to keep a brochure on budget.

- CONSIDER GOING WITH A LOWER GRADE OF PAPER. Depending on the project, a lower grade might work well and save money.

- BUY PAPER DIRECT FROM THE PAPER COMPANY. Though your printer may not be crazy about this choice—because it reduces his profits—it can cut costs when you're really struggling to meet a client's budget.

- EXPLORE DIGITAL PRINTING. Depending on the design specifics and print-run size, digital might be a more cost-effective option than offset printing. Just be sure you ask questions about the capabilities—and limitations—of any digital printer you choose.

WHOLESALELIFE
INSURANCE BROKERAGE

| COMPANY | INDIVIDUAL | BUSINESS |

INNOVATIVE SOLUTIONS
UNIQUELY TARGETED
FOR YOUR BUSINESS

| COMPANY | INDIVIDUAL | **BUSINESS** |

Settlement of Existing Policies
In certain instances, it may
make sense to explore the
value of your current policies.
Our expertise in the active
secondary insurance market
allows us to shop any of your
existing policies and procure
the best offer available.

NEW LIFE INSURANCE
As a business owner, no one knows your business better than
you. But no one knows how to protect your business better than
Wholesale Life. We are dedicated to understanding the intricacies
of your company as well as your plans for your financial future. Our
experienced staff and industry expertise allow us to provide insurance strategies designed to protect every aspect of your business
while growing your solid financial foundation. Utilizing various types
of products and our direct-to-you model, we can provide the most
comprehensive coverage for your business at the lowest prices.

NEXT GENERATION PREMIUM FINANCED PRODUCTS
The cost of insurance for an independent business owner can be
exorbitant. We understand the importance of guarding your cash
flow while protecting your business. Utilizing the Next Generation
of Premium Financing we can design a solution that meets your
unique business requirements while carefully controlling your
out-of-pocket costs.

Wholesale Life Insurance Brokerage understands that as the owner
of a thriving business, you have dedicated yourself to the growth
and success of your company. In order to protect everything you
have built, we have developed a series of strategies designed to
specifically meet the needs of individual business owners. These
premier customized strategies protect you, your business and your
financial health.

ACCOUNTS RECEIVABLE FINANCING
For many businesses, the advantages of
accounts receivable financing may be the key
to successful financial planning, including
Deferred Compensation, Exit Strategies,
and Wealth Creation. This new strategy of
monetizing an unrealized asset transfers
your company's accounts receivables into
compound growth without factoring or
interrupting your day-to-day operations or
cash flow. This leveraged compensation
arrangement is designed to convert the value
of your dormant asset into an income-
producing asset while providing a level of
protection from liability exposure.

SELF-FUNDING OPTIONS
For some business owners, self-funding their
life insurance is an attractive and sensible
option. Wholesale Life is the leader in creative
strategies that provides protection while
mitigating tax liabilities. Our creative strategies
include Business Equity-based programs or
solutions that utilize the U.S. Dollar or the
more attractive Japanese Yen.

**SELF-EQUITY PREMIUM FINANCING
STRATEGIES INCLUDE:**
• 100% Self-Pay Premium Financing
• Bank Financed Premium Financing
    • United States Dollar based
    • Japanese Yen based
• Business Equity-based Premium Financing with a Letter of Credit
• Estate Equity-based Premium Financing with a Letter of Credit

▲ *The Rule29 designers kept this brochure
inexpensive by choosing a digital printer.
They also gave it a more upscale feel
with rounded corners. To keep this detail
affordable, the corners were ground off rather
than die-cut.*

► *When you're working with a charitable
organization—such as this Food for the
Hungry brochure—Justin Ahrens at Rule29
suggests telling the printer. They might be
more willing to work with you on price when
it benefits a good cause.*

make a
difference
in the fight
against world
poverty

...become a
Food for the Hungry
advocate

Food for
the Hungry

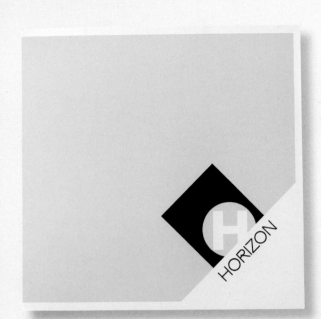

◄▼ To maximize the budget, Rule29 designers reverse engineered this brochure's size with the printer to get the most out of the press sheet. An innovative fold—the brochure doubles in width twice as you unfold it—along with bold colors and graphics work together to form a lasting impression.

Low-Cost Artwork

With a budget-conscious brochure, there's rarely enough money for original photography, but a little DIY elbow grease can put you in control of the artwork without breaking the bank. Scalin, for example, might create an illustration for a brochure he's designing—but only when his style meshes well with the client and project. He'll also shoot original photography for a brochure when the image needs to fall within his skill set. This approach simply adds design hours to a project rather than the high cost of an outside vendor.

There's also a wealth of inexpensive stock photography available when you can't hire a photographer. It's fairly quick and easy to search through any number of royalty-free options online. But the Web has also given birth to a new copyright model called Creative Commons (http://creativecommons. org). It allows everyone from photographers to scientists to share their work under a variety of alternative copyrights. Some, for example, allow use with attribution, while others restrict sharing to noncommercial purposes. On Flickr (www.flickr.com), some users mark their image sets to a Creative Commons copyright for various levels of sharing.

Depending on a project's subject matter, there may be other options for free, high-quality imagery. Donna McGrath, a design manager at Rand McNally in Skokie, Illinois, often taps the resources of convention and visitors bureaus for the company's travel-related projects. These groups often have great professional-quality photography available for the asking. A simple Google search may also turn up low- or no-cost imagery. One example is Stock.XCHNG (www.sxc. hu) where photographers upload their images to share with others for little or no cost, though sometimes small restrictions apply.

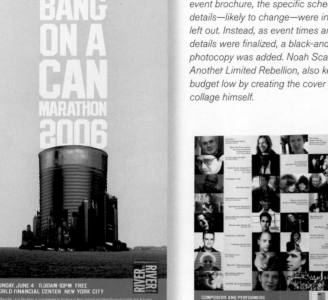

◄▼ *To get more mileage out of this music-event brochure, the specific scheduling details—likely to change—were intentionally left out. Instead, as event times and other details were finalized, a black-and-white photocopy was added. Noah Scalin, of Another Limited Rebellion, also kept the budget low by creating the cover photo collage himself.*

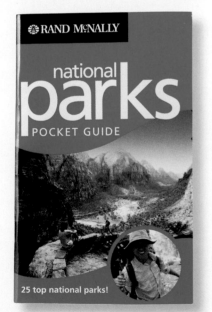

▲ *Since there wasn't a budget for original photography, Rand McNally's in-house design team needed to figure out how to make existing photography fresh for this National Parks Pocket Guide. Interesting crops—such as the circular one shown here—help keep the imagery engaging.*

▼ *Donna McGrath, a design manager at Rand McNally, put this travel booklet together on a tight timeframe and budget. To acquire free photography, she tapped convention and visitors bureaus along with specific attractions featured in the book. Museums and other tourist sites are often happy to provide high-quality imagery at no cost.*

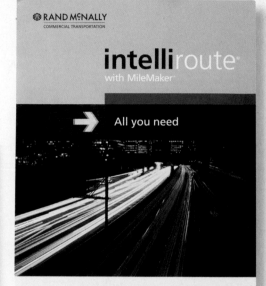

▲ *Rand McNally's in-house design team saved money on this brochure—handed out at a trade show—by picking up the same graphics used for the booth design. This technique also created a cohesive branding message.*

THINGS TO KNOW

BE YOUR OWN STOCK AGENCY

It's a cringe-worthy moment: you spot the same royalty-free image you used for a client's brochure two months later on a highway billboard. But when there's no budget for original photography, it can feel like you're stuck choosing from the same low-cost images as everyone else. So what's an enterprising designer to do?

Become your own stock agency. Or, put more simply, start taking your digital camera with you wherever you go. Snap pictures of that funny sign at your favorite Chinese restaurant. Capture the line of cars in front of you when traffic is at a complete standstill. In fact, take a picture of anything that catches your eye—without giving too much thought to when or if you'll use the image.

With a little diligence, you can create a photography habit that turns into an image library that is thousands strong. You'll likely find yourself paying more attention to the details of everyday life and bringing those varied inspirations into your design work. Plus, your new image library will serve as a powerful idea bank. Scan through it to help you find ideas for texture or mood. And the next time there's a nonexistent photography budget, you may discover the perfect image living right on your hard drive, one you know won't unexpectedly show up on a billboard.

PLANNING | DESIGN BASICS | **BUDGET CONSIDERATIONS** | PRACTICAL MATTERS

DESIGN MATTERS // BROCHURES 01

PRACTIC
MATTER

AL
S

"IT'S IMPORTANT TO PAY ATTENTION TO DETAILS. THE MORE DETAIL ORIENTED YOU CAN BE ON A PIECE, THE MORE VALUABLE YOU WILL BE TO AN ART DIRECTOR OR CLIENT." –LOUIS JOHNSON, SENIOR DESIGNER AT IRON DESIGN

SO YOU'RE FINALLY DONE. YOU'VE GOT THE PERFECT BROCHURE DESIGN SITTING RIGHT THERE ON YOUR COMPUTER SCREEN. IT'S GORGEOUS, AND FUNCTIONAL, AND SMART. IT HITS ALL THE STRATEGIC SWEET SPOTS. UNFORTUNATELY, HAVING AN IMPRESSIVE DESIGN ON YOUR MONITOR ISN'T THE SAME AS HOLDING A STUNNING PIECE IN YOUR HANDS. "IT MIGHT LOOK GREAT ON YOUR SCREEN," SAYS SAMANTHA REITMAYER, A PRINCIPAL AT ROVILLO + REITMAYER IN DALLAS. "BUT WHAT ABOUT THE PRODUCT?"

Getting it Printed

To get from a design on your computer to a beautiful printed piece, you have to navigate a number of crucial steps and avoid countless pitfalls along the way. Whether it's a color that's off or a special effect gone wrong, there's nothing worse than having a surprise after you've printed 20,000 copies. "There are a million ways for things to go wrong," says Paul Wharton, vice president, creative, at Larsen in Minneapolis. As such, it's key to follow up on every production detail. Reitmayer couldn't agree more. "I think you have to babysit it every step of the way," she says about print projects. "You have to develop a good relationship with your printer. Find someone good who you like, and likes you, and learn from them." Early in her career, she developed a loyalty to a particular printer and picked up a great deal of knowledge from the connection.

How can you safeguard against a misstep? Do as much homework as possible in advance. "A key way to not make mistakes is to sit down with the printer and show him your design and say, 'Do you see any problems?'" Wharton says. If you want to take this a step further, make an actual mock-up of your design using the paper you want to print it on. This gives you a chance to spot any pitfalls and creates another communication tool for the production process. "Take it to the printer and bindery company," Reitmayer says. "Make sure it's possible. And see what it costs." After talking with the printer, you may be surprised at what you can and can't afford. Don't be afraid to ask questions.

Special Effects

When they're chosen carefully—and executed well—special processes elevate brochure projects to another level. These extra touches can help grab people's attention and keep it, but to do so, they need to be applied judiciously. "Doing something just for the sake of doing it doesn't make sense," Wharton says. "One of the rules of thumb would be, 'Does the special process enhance the message?'" Adding a foil stamp to a brochure cover just for decoration, for instance, probably isn't such a good idea. But if it communicates the upscale nature of the business, you're reinforcing a key brand attribute.

It's also a challenge to make sure your chosen effect turns out the way you imagine. Whether you're considering embossing or foil stamping, there are strengths and limitations to each process. You need to know what those are and plan appropriately. These processes all add weight to the type or artwork—something to keep in mind during the design process. This is another instance where it pays to work closely with your vendor and learn as much as you can about the technique in advance of printing. Here's a closer look at some popular options:

FOIL STAMPING

When they started working on a promotional brochure for RSVP Soirée, a catering and event rental company, the design team at Rovillo + Reitmayer knew they had to send a distinctive message. The client's target audience was an upscale, exclusive crowd, so the piece needed to feel high-end. So how did they grab attention? In part, it was with a gold foil stamp displayed prominently on the cover. This shiny effect contrasts with the uncoated brown cover stock to create a bold contrast. "It's something people want to touch and feel," Reitmayer says. "It makes it a little harder to throw away."

► *This series of brochures promotes Wausau Paper's capabilities as applied to five different business segments: hospitality, industrial, banking, public institutions, and retail. Each folder focuses on a different special process and includes sample projects—such as a business card, invitation, and brochure— tucked in the front. Larsen in Minneapolis designed this project.*

In essence, the foil stamp adds another dimension to this brochure and makes it more likely that people will want to explore the piece. If you're considering a foil stamp for a future project, Reitmayer recommends getting in touch with the vendor and sharing your artwork. She says you can run type as small as six or seven points and still achieve a beautiful effect, but it's still a good idea to let the printer take a look. Another must? "Samples are great, but if you really want to know what a black foil stamp is going to look like on that Eames paper, get them to do that," she says. Most vendors are happy to test specific foil on your chosen paper.

Taking the time to test is much better than being disappointed with the results. "Not every paper takes foil well," Wharton says. Since there are a wide variety of foils in a rainbow of colors, make sure you choose carefully. Ask for the foil you've chosen to be tested on the actual paper you want to use because some foils, for instance, fill in. You can avoid unnecessary hand wringing with a quick check.

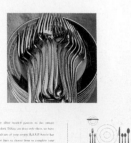

◄▼ A gold foil stamp on the cover of this catering and rental company brochure makes it feel special—a feeling continued inside with touches of metallic ink. "It adds another dimension," says Samantha Reitmayer, principal of Rovillo + Reitmayer in Dallas.

DIE CUTTING

This may very well be one of the most functional special printing effects. You can use a die cut to make things slide together or create an interesting interplay—say between a cover and the first page. Often, you're creating an interesting window to what lies beneath, sort of a commercial for the interior or next layer. But although die cutting can create interesting effects, Wharton says it's key to keep in mind that this isn't necessarily a highly refined technique.

"You can die cut some pretty interesting shapes," he says. "But they're like a cookie cutter. They're cutting it out." And since no die has a perfect edge, this process often leaves little nicks, especially when you're cutting a more intricate shape. The die, for instance, likely punches completely out a simple circle, with the excess paper falling to the floor. A more complex shape, however, isn't completely cut out by the die and needs to be knocked the rest of the way out at the end of the line. The resulting nicks can be ground off or shaved off, but you have to know they're going to happen in order to plan on how to deal with them.

▲▶ Minneapolis-based Larsen designed this piece for Wausau Paper to show how the company's products can be used in conjunction with die cutting. The design team created actual samples, including a business card and fold-up box, to demonstrate the technique. It's part of a series of brochures on different processes.

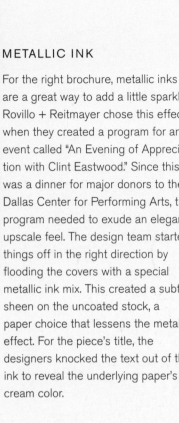

METALLIC INK

For the right brochure, metallic inks are a great way to add a little sparkle. Rovillo + Reitmayer chose this effect when they created a program for an event called "An Evening of Appreciation with Clint Eastwood." Since this was a dinner for major donors to the Dallas Center for Performing Arts, the program needed to exude an elegant, upscale feel. The design team started things off in the right direction by flooding the covers with a special metallic ink mix. This created a subtle sheen on the uncoated stock, a paper choice that lessens the metallic effect. For the piece's title, the designers knocked the text out of the ink to reveal the underlying paper's cream color.

▲◄ *With a special metallic ink mix on the cover, this program exudes a luxe feel. Dallas design firm Rovillo + Reitmayer wanted the piece to feel upscale, because it was being given out at a dinner for major donors to the Dallas Center for the Performing Arts. A mix of three different paper stocks makes the piece a pleasure to hold and explore. To break up information, the design team decided to put some of the text onto cards that slide out from the inside of the front and back covers.*

Thinking about metallic ink? Make sure you know how it will set up on your chosen paper. It's probably a good idea to ask your printer to do an ink draw down that will show you how the ink and paper work together. (Reitmayer recommends doing this test anytime you're dealing with an unfamiliar paper or ink.) In general, metallic ink tends to set up better—and look more metallic—on coated paper. It also has the potential to scratch when printed in large swaths, which tends to be more noticeable on smooth paper than textured. To prevent blemishes, Reitmayer recommends a protective varnish or aqueous coating. There are newer metallic inks that don't require coatings, but they tend to be more expensive. When in doubt, talk with your printer about how to keep your metallics looking perfect and shiny.

Founding Families

Ruth and Ken Altshuler

Doris Bass, the Harry W. Bass, Jr. Foundation

Boeckman Family, through the Boeckman Family & JFM Foundations

Christine and Eric Brauss

Diane and Hal Brierley

Toni and Norman Brinker

Nancy and Clint Carlson

Mary Anne and Richard Cree

Linda and Bill Custard and Frank Pitts

Arlene and John Dayton

Brad Dyer

Rosemary and Roger Enrico

Amy and Vernon Faulconer

Candice and Robert Haas

Fanchon and Howard Hallam

Caroline Rose Hunt

Gene and Jerry Jones

Kim Hiett Jordan

Barbara and Mark Lemmon

Joy and Ronald Mankoff

Nancy Cain Marcus

Phyllis and Tom McCasland

Mrs. Eugene McDermott

Juanita and Henry S. Miller, Jr. and the Miller Family

Dana and Charles Nearburg

Angela Paulos and the Paulos Family

Sarah and Ross Perot, Jr.

Nelda Cain Pickens

Caren Prothro, through the Vin and Caren Prothro Family Foundation

Deedie and Rusty Rose

Sarah and Charles Seay

Stemmons Family, through the Stemmons Foundation

Ted Strauss and the Strauss Family

Margaret and Jack Sweet

Debbie and John Tolleson

Ellen and Don Williams

Jean Wilson

Margot and Bill Winspear

Mary and Bob Wright

Dee and Charles Wyly

Cheryl and Sam Wyly

Anonymous Founding Families (4)

Cornerstone Donors

Alon USA

Bank of America

Jane and Ron Beneke Family

Robert H. Dedman Family

Jan and Fred Hegi and the Hegi Family

Cinda and Tom Hicks

JPMorgan Chase

J.L. and Sydney Thweatt Huffines

Jerry R. Junkins Family Foundation

The Irvin L. Levy and Kenneth L. Schnitzer Families

Nancy and Kenton McGee, Alexandra and Robert Lavie and The McGee Foundation

Virginia and Robert Payne Family

Margot and Ross Perot

Boone Pickens

Caren H. Prothro

The Meadows Foundation

The Murchison Family

Cindy and Howard Rachofsky

Jan and Trevor Rees-Jones

Peggy and Leonard Riggs

Sue Gill Rose

Peggy and Carl Sewell

Annette and Harold Simmons

Jane and Bud Smith

Gayle and Paul Stoffel

Bea and Ray Wallace

Donna Wilhelm

Kathy and Rodney Woods

Anonymous

Founding Corporations and Foundations

American Airlines

Brinker International

Communities Foundation of Texas

Dallas Leadership Banking Partnership

Dean Foods

EDS

Flagship Corporate Alliance

Kimberly-Clark

Landmark Foundation Partnership

Eugene McDermott Foundation

Nokia

Once Upon a Time Foundation

Perkins-Prothro Foundation

Rosewood Foundation

Texas Instruments Foundation

TXU

Elsa Von Seggern Foundation

EMBOSSING

This technique allows you literally to raise parts of your design to another level. Maybe you want to elevate and emphasize a company's name on a brochure cover or give extra oomph to an illustration. "An emboss should be used to enhance the design or message," Wharton says. "It is used most effectively when you're trying to do something very subtle or to give something more impact than it would have any other way." A blind emboss, for instance, should highlight the beauty of the substrate, while an embossing used in conjunction with printing needs to enhance, rather than detract from, the printing.

To make sure the process goes well, Wharton recommends getting the printer or embosser involved early in the process. You should involve these professional partners in the planning process to prevent designing something that is difficult or impossible to produce. It's also key to ask for samples and understand what kind of embosses a particular vendor offers. Will it be sculpted or single-level? What about the bevel? These can vary greatly in depth and width. Ask these questions in advance, so you're not disappointed with the final product.

Wharton worked on a Wausau paper promotion with a potato chip character on the cover that was highlighted with a sculptured emboss.

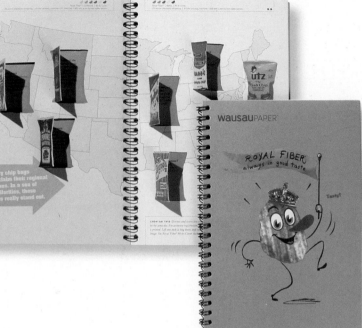

This technique literally gives the potato chip ripples and defines details on the crown, which includes a gold foil. For this piece, Wharton created a diagram to show exactly how he wanted things to come out, noting which parts should be up, down, and rounded. He also sent the printer a sticker from a commercial stationery set to show the depth and detail of embossing he wanted to achieve. In other instances, he has sent actual objects, such as a shell, and told the vendor he wanted the embossing to look as much like the 3D item as possible.

▲ *Designers at Larsen in Minneapolis made this potato chip character come alive with a sculptured emboss. To make sure it came out as they envisioned, they sent detailed instructions to the printer along with a sample emboss showing the quality they wanted to achieve. This piece promotes Wausau Paper's Royal Fiber line through a story about regional potato chips, showing designers throughout the book exactly how the paper holds up to special techniques.*

WHEN YOU'RE MAKING A PAPER AIRPLANE TO LOB OVER A CUBICLE WALL, IT DOESN'T MATTER IF THOSE FOLDS COME WITH A FEW CRINKLES AND WRINKLES. A BROCHURE, ON THE OTHER HAND, REQUIRES THE SAME LEVEL OF ARTISTRY AS AN ORIGAMI CRANE. YOU NEED TO PAY ATTENTION TO ALL THE TECHNICAL DETAILS TO ACHIEVE CLEAN AND PERFECT CREASES. IT'S AN ESSENTIAL TOPIC TO BRING UP WITH YOUR PRINTER BEFORE A PIECE HITS THE PRESS.

Press Checks and Folding

Louis Johnson, a senior designer at Iron Design in Ithaca, New York, says it's key to pay attention to whether a piece folds grain long or grain short. When the fold runs grain long—parallel to the fibers in the paper—it reduces the risk of cracking. "It took me a long time to get that little rule down," he says. "You should just be sure to tell the printer you want it to be produced to reduce the cracking in the fold." If you have solid, flat colors, for instance, cracks stand out because they can cause white paper to show through.

It's also crucial to attend press checks to make sure the colors come out the way you want. Johnson attended two different checks for a brochure he worked on to promote the city of Ithaca to businesses. He suggests taking a proof with you to the press check and working with the printer to get the color as accurate as possible. "It's tricky," he says. "You have to discuss it within the four-color process." If something is off, you might ask to add more yellow, but a qualified printer can also bring ideas to the table, perhaps suggesting you reduce the cyan instead.

For Johnson's Ithaca brochure, it was especially crucial to match colors. There were large swaths of color that ran across spreads, and the left and right pages didn't necessarily get printed on the exact same print run. "You have to rely on your eyes," he says. "And know when to pick your battles." In this piece, for instance, he describes the colors as 95 percent close to his ideal. He didn't push those background shades to more exacting standards because he felt it would compromise the quality of the photographs.

In the end, the key to mastering production is bringing out your inner Martha Stewart. "It's important to pay attention to details," he says. "The more detail-oriented you can be on a piece, the more valuable you will be to an art director or client." Becoming a stickler builds trust—and that's definitely a good thing.

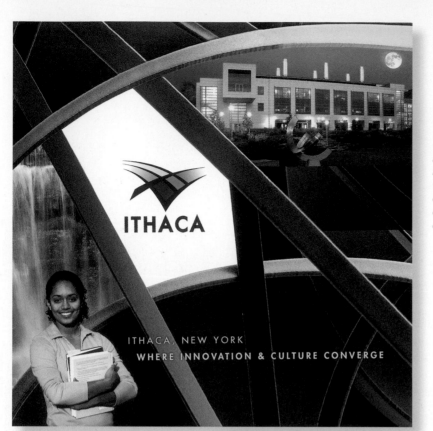

◄▼ Since images bleed across spreads, Louis Johnson, senior designer at Iron Design in Ithaca, New York, needed to work with the printer to make sure the folds were exact. He also attended two press checks to oversee color. This brochure promotes the city of Ithaca to businesses.

Choosing Paper

"I always start with the papers," says Samantha Reitmayer, a principal at Rovillo + Reitmayer. "Before I even start with the design, I'm thinking tactilely." So drag out the swatch books and paper samples and spend a few minutes thinking about how touching a particular stock is going to make someone feel. And more importantly, how does the piece need to feel? Glossy? Rich?

For the Clint Eastwood program, for example, the team at Rovillo + Reitmayer mixed together several different stocks for a luxurious experience. The cover stock is folded over on itself, creating a thick cover that feels important. Just inside the front and back covers, there's a semitrans- lucent sheet with a texture similar to rice paper, creating an impressive entrance and exit for the brochure. The main pages are on a smooth, un- coated stock that contrasts nicely with the textured cover. Together, these three paper stocks make exploring the program a lavish undertaking.

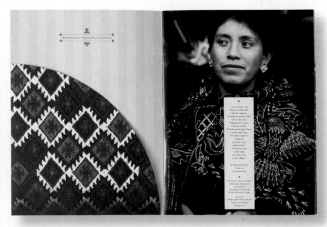

▲◄ *Getting all the production details just right elevates a brochure to another level. For this fundraising piece, Dallas design firm Rovillo + Reitmayer chose an uncoated, textured stock for the cover. It feels good in the hand, holds color well, and creates a nice contrast to the coated stock inside.*

DOUBLE VISION

Take a quick look at this brochure's cover and it seems pretty straightforward. It's a trade show piece highlighting road services along Croatian motorways. But take a closer gander—or move the cover back and forth in your hands—and you'll find yourself momentarily mesmerized. Thanks to lenticular printing, the three square signs across the middle of the cover change displays just like the real thing.

"Special printing effects add another dimension to the design in an attractive and bold way," says Marko Rašic, a designer with Studio Rašic. In this case, he believes the animation adds a sense of time. The effect is particularly appropriate because it highlights the only element that all Croatian motorways have in common—electronic signs with changing displays. The technique's use also creates a sense of continuity with previous pieces for this client, where lenticular printing was also used to reinforce the concept.

So how do you know when it's appropriate to use such a head-turning technique? "It is important that we don't use those special printing effects just to pump up the piece and fascinate someone only with effects," he says. "One should always keep in mind that the effect has to, conceptually and design-wise, complement the idea and the whole layout." Just like the changing speed limits and driver warnings on the cover of this brochure.

► *Studio Rašic used lenticular printing on this brochure's cover to highlight the electronic signs, which are the only element all Croatian motorways have in common.*

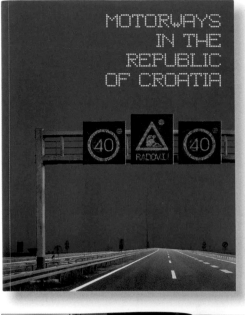

MIX AND MATCH

When St. Louis design firm Kuhlmann Leavitt started working on this capabilities brochure, they knew there wasn't enough room in the budget for original photography. But the design team still needed to figure out a way to help its client, consulting group Collaborative Strategies, attract attention. Instead of turning to stock photography, the design firm decided to add color and variety with a simple printing trick: They chose a small rainbow of uncoated stock for the piece's interior and one ink color, black.

Mixing and matching these warm shades of paper adds personality and appeal to the brochure without busting the project's small budget. From there, it's all about the type and a few simple diagrams. Black copy presented in Helvetica Bold makes a striking statement on the colored stock, while the diagrams help illustrate key concepts. The book's title, Get Collaborative, plays off the client's website address and sums up the company's working strategy. It's an effective, affordable brochure that proves that less sometimes really is more.

▶ *Mixing different colors of uncoated paper stock helps this brochure make an impact without a single photograph.*

SIX TIPS FOR CHOOSING THE RIGHT PAPER

Stop flipping aimlessly through those swatch books and try these tactics for choosing the perfect paper every time:

··· **MAKE IT MATCH.** You wouldn't wear brown socks with black shoes, so don't choose a paper that fights with a brochure's overall concept. It's nearly impossible to select the right stock—one that reinforces a project's central idea—until you've completed the initial problem-solving phase. Though in some cases, a certain paper can spark a solution and become a central part of the concept.

··· **SEND THE RIGHT MESSAGE.** If you're doing a brochure for an exclusive consumer product, you probably don't want to print it on thin, flimsy stock. All the beauty shots in the world can't counteract the message sent by a piece that feels cheap when you pick it up.

··· **LEAN ON YOUR PRINTER.** Before you take a paper choice to a client, take a few minutes to run it by a trusted printer. Do you need to emboss? Fold? Withstand the abuse of mail delivery? He or she can give you a good idea whether a given stock will pass muster.

··· **THINK ABOUT TOUCH.** Have you considered how a given paper will feel in people's hands? Do you want them to run their fingers over slick coated stock or enjoy something sensuous? A textured, uncoated stock might provide a more tactile experience—if that's what you're trying to achieve.

··· **CONSIDER AN UPGRADE.** Are you doing a small print run? Then explore upgrading to a nicer stock. If you don't need much paper to begin with, this choice isn't likely to bust the budget, but it can help the project stand out.

··· **BEFRIEND YOUR PAPER REP.** If you take the time to build a relationship, your paper rep can help you out when you're in a bind. Can't quite find what you're looking for? He or she can probably recommend some viable options.

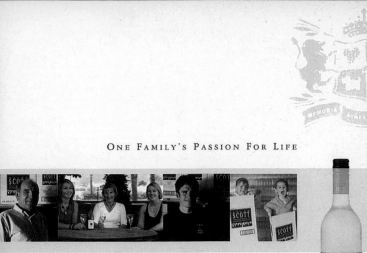

ONE FAMILY'S PASSION FOR LIFE

GENERATION AFTER GENERATION

◀▼ *For this winery brochure, Alex Lloyd of Lloyds Graphic Design Limited in Blenheim, New Zealand, chose crisp, white, textured stock for an upscale feel. A coated stock would have been at odds with the winery's natural feel and past marketing efforts. "It's not a glitzy, glossy place," Lloyd says.*

ALLAN AND JOSHUA

CONTINUING HERITAGE... TRADITION IN THE MAKING

ALLAN SCOTT

Coming from a Canterbury farming family, Allan's first contact with the wine industry came in 1973 as an employee of a major wine company, assisting with the original vine plantings in Marlborough. After several years managing a major vineyard, he resigned to head a national viticultural team for another wine company. In this role, Allan developed an interest in the winemaking process as well. This interest eventually led to the establishment of Allan Scott Wines and Estates Ltd.

An associated business of contract grape growing and a busy viticultural consultancy were the early background to the company, with Allan being instrumental in the development of many of the region's vineyards along with localized vineyard husbandry techniques. Allan's key role as Director of the company is to manage production and sales aspects along with the coordination of all facets of the business.

CATHERINE SCOTT

Catherine is one of the few personnel of the Marlborough wine industry who was born and bred in the province. A fifth generation Marlburian, she also comes from a farming family. She trained as a nurse at Wairau Hospital, Marlborough and nursed in Christchurch. Having travelled extensively with a good eye for detail, Catherine has a discerning palate and plays an important role in the winemaking team. As a Director, she takes an all-encompassing responsibility for all aspects of administration, and management of the cellar door and restaurant.

JOSHUA, VICTORIA & SARA SCOTT

Today Allan Scott Wines is a truly family business - with son Josh as winemaker, daughter Victoria runs the restaurant / cellar door while younger daughter Sara has her Winemaking diploma with local and international winemaking experience.

LEFT TO RIGHT:
VICTORIA, CATHERINE AND SARA

CASE S

TUDIES

"IF YOU SIT IN THE MIDDLE OF THE ROAD, IT'S A SCARY PLACE TO BE. YOU GET RUN OVER." —PUM LEFEBURE, CREATIVE DIRECTOR AT DESIGN ARMY

THE CLIENT: THE WALTERS ART MUSEUM

DESIGN FIRM: PRINCIPLE

The Walters Art Museum

DESIGNING FOR THE RIGHT AUDIENCE

Sometimes the best way to kick off a project is by taking a hard look at its previous incarnation. When Principle started working with the Walters Art Museum on a brochure for its school programs, Allyson Lack, a partner at the design firm, studied the existing piece's primary colors and glossy paper. "It was very much what comes to mind when you think of young children," she says.

But for school programs, it's the teachers, not the students, who sign their classes up for outings at the Baltimore museum—a fact that meant the project's target audience consisted primarily of 25- to 40-year-old women. So Lack pitched an entirely different approach: "Let's make it more sophisticated." The resulting brochure feels more like a program handed out at the symphony than something found at a grade school.

The piece's white, uncoated paper gives it a refined feel, while the brown text and illustrations keep it soft. Interior pages pair copy about planning a visit with the gorgeous artwork that teachers and students might see at the museum. To make sure these rich, colorful paintings reproduced well, Principle chose a stochastic printing method—its randomized dot pattern results in a tighter image. The brochure also features stock line art, which Lack found to represent items in one of the museum's exhibits.

▲ This brochure highlights school programs at the Walters Art Museum in Baltimore, Maryland. Since teachers make up the target audience, designers at Principle created a sophisticated—rather than kid-centric—design. Brown type gives this piece a warm feel without detracting from the gorgeous paintings.

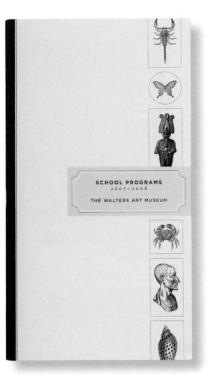

In the middle of the brochure, there is something just for students: a full-sized poster is folded and bound into the piece. Teachers can pull it out and hang it up in their classrooms for their students to enjoy. The poster is covered with line art that corresponds to objects at the Walters Art Museum, so it gives students something to get excited about before they step in the door.

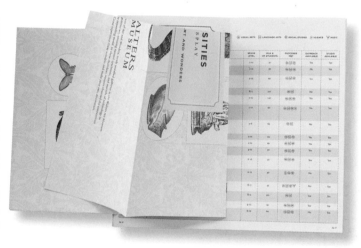

▲► To give the brochure additional value, there's a full-size poster bound in the center. Teachers can take it out and hang it up in their classrooms to get students excited about visiting the museum. The front side of the poster features line art that corresponds with items students might see during a visit. On the back, they can read about each curiosity.

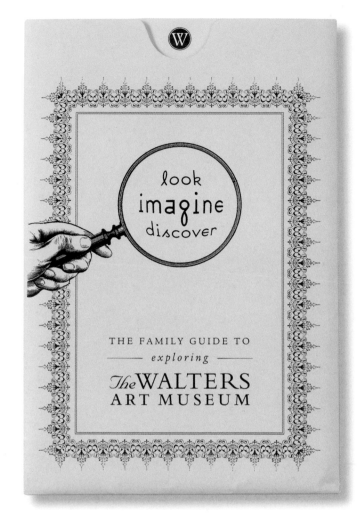

◄ A twist on the standard brochure, this sleeve and the set of cards inside help families enjoy the Walters Art Museum. Multiple pieces mean there's no reason for siblings to fight over a single brochure.

This piece went so well that Principle was also tapped to create a family guide for the museum. The new project needed to be equally fun and engaging for parents and their kids. After some brainstorming, the design team and museum staff settled on the idea of a deck of cards. This format makes a visit to the museum feel like a game designed for the whole family. A mom can hand a card or two to each of her kids—no fighting over a single brochure.

To keep things kid-friendly, Principle made the cards fairly large—8 $\frac{7}{8}$ x 5 $\frac{5}{8}$-inches (22.5 x 14.3 cm)—and printed them on sturdy 80 lb. stock. Each card features a different item for families to find in the museum and the entire set slips easily into a sleeve. There's also an introductory card in large type that explains how to use the deck, making the copy more accessible for young readers. Much like a deck of standard playing cards, rounded corners also give the set a friendly feel.

◄ *Each card features a different object for families to find together in the museum. To make them kid friendly, the cards are fairly large at 8 ⅞ x 5 ⅝ inches (22.5 x 14.3 cm) and printed on sturdy 80 lb. (36.28739 kg) stock.*

The outer sleeve was created from a lighter weight paper, so Lack needed to make sure the glue used to hold it together wouldn't seep through. It also features a thumb notch at the top for ease of use, which also serves as a subtle branding element with the Walters logo showing through from the top card. The front features a magnifying glass, which hints at the scavenger hunt nature of the cards inside.

For the cards themselves, Principle kept things bright and fun, choosing a different color for each one. These highlight a picture of an artifact on the front side along with a brief description of the item. The back includes additional details about the art along with questions for a family to discuss together. This approach allows different age groups to enjoy the piece together. Small children can simply look for the object in the picture, while older kids can read the copy and initiate discussions with their parents.

GO TO THE CHARLES ST. BUILDING,
LEVEL 2, 18TH- & 19TH-CENTURY TREASURY

FABERGÉ EGG

Given as an Easter gift to the former Czarina (*zar-ee-na*) or queen, of Russia by her son Nicholas II, this egg is decorated with gold and pearls and is one of only 56 imperial Easter eggs. It opens to reveal a perfect miniature replica of a royal palace in Russia.

THE FAMILY GUIDE
— **FABERGÉ EGG** —

look

As part of a family tradition, the Czar (*tzar*) or king, had an artist create an egg shaped gift to give both his mother and his wife at Easter. See if you can find the cannon, the flag, the statue, and the trees. Look for other things you recognize and point them out to the people with you.

imagine

Discuss some of your own family traditions with the people who are with you. For what occasions do you give gifts to friends and family members? What kind of surprise would you give as a gift? Why?

You act as an artist when you create something to give to another. You have the choice to make it large or small. Which is more difficult to create? Why do you say that?

discover

Decorated eggs have been a symbol of life and spring since ancient times. Ancient Egyptians and Persians dyed eggs in spring colors and gave them to friends as gifts.

➔ **COLLECTION CONNECTION** ←

Henry Walters gave his entire collection of art to the city of Baltimore when he died. Everything in this museum should be considered a gift to the citizens of the city by Mr. Walters.

◄ *"Even if little kids can't read yet, they can still hold up a bright yellow card and look for a Fabergé egg," says Allyson Lack, a partner at Principle. For older children, the back of each card gives information about the item and questions to talk about with parents. Large, legible type keeps things accessible for young readers.*

THE CLIENT: KNOLL

DESIGN FIRM: GIAMPIETRO+SMITH

Knoll Space

A LITTLE PACKAGE PACKS A BIG PUNCH

"How can we make a piece as structurally interesting as the furniture itself?"

—Rob Giampietro, principal, Giampietro+Smith

Though it's relatively small in scale, this brochure needed to make a lasting impression: It kicked off a new brand called Knoll Space. The legendary furniture company wanted to make select pieces from its studio line normally sold through architects and interior designers available directly to the public. So the company turned to New York design firm Giampietro+Smith to help launch this venture.

The firm worked on everything from the name and attributes of the new brand to the look and feel of the introductory print piece. One name considered was Knoll Home, but ultimately, it didn't make sense to associate the line with a name that would limit the base of potential customers. Apartment dwellers might be just

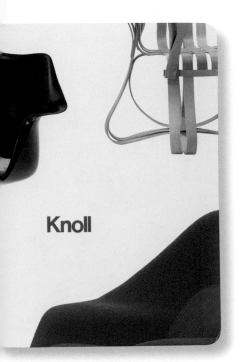

▲ New York firm Giampietro+Smith put together this brochure to help launch Knoll Space, a selection of Knoll furniture sold directly to consumers. Since they needed to work with existing photography, the design team created interesting crops with the cover imagery to help distinguish this new brand.

as likely to splurge on a womb chair as traditional homeowners. Plus, the line includes office furniture as well as residential pieces.

But perhaps an even bigger challenge than naming the brand was creating a brochure that lived up to its contents. "How can we make a piece as structurally interesting as the furniture itself?" says Rob Giampietro, principal of Giampietro+Smith. It's a tough question to answer when you're working with furniture designed by such icons as Frank Gehry and Ludwig Mies van der Rohe.

The firm had recently finished another project with an accordion fold, so after some brainstorming, the design team decided to use the same technique for this piece. The accordion fold gives the piece a sculptural feel, one that makes consumers want to keep the brochure once they pick it up at a retailer such as Design Within Reach. This approach also gives a nod to the exquisite forms of the furniture featured in the line.

The spreads on the front side of the brochure pair furniture beauty shots with approachable copy that establishes the brand's personality. This section introduces consumers to Knoll's history and lets them know what to expect from Knoll Space with such lines as: "Surround yourself with beauty. Invest in innovation." On the back, the brochure becomes a mini product catalog with small, labeled images of the pieces offered in the Knoll Space collection.

Celebrated architects and designers from around the world have worked with Knoll for decades to shape offices, hotels and museums. Now, these collaborations will help to shape the contemporary home. Knoll Space offers unparalleled quality that can only come from Knoll.

Define your home with imagination, vision and insight. Nothing is more classic—more timeless—than modern design. With Knoll Space, it's more available than ever before.

Knoll Space
Surround yourself with beauty. Invest in innovation.

◄ The piece's accordion fold makes it feel like a sculpture—a nod to the exquisite forms of the furniture shown within the brochure.

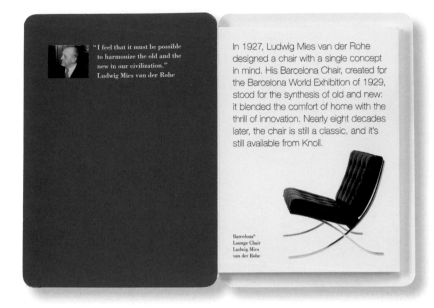

In 1927, Ludwig Mies van der Rohe designed a chair with a single concept in mind. His Barcelona Chair, created for the Barcelona World Exhibition of 1929, stood for the synthesis of old and new: it blended the comfort of home with the thrill of innovation. Nearly eight decades later, the chair is still a classic, and it's still available from Knoll.

"I feel that it must be possible to harmonize the old and the new in our civilization."
Ludwig Mies van der Rohe

Barcelona®
Lounge Chair
Ludwig Mies
van der Rohe

► *Interior pages are slightly smaller than the front and back covers, giving the piece a feel similar to a hardcover book. Die-cut from a single sheet of paper, the piece was folded at the printer.*

Since project parameters didn't allow for original photography, designers worked hard to make existing imagery create its own statement. They put an emphasis on individual pieces of furniture instead of beauty shots of a room and used both silhouetting and cropping to help distinguish the brand. In the catalog section, for instance, individual chairs face different directions to simulate how you might find them in a room. "We wanted things to feel like they're conversing with each other," Giampietro says. The designers stripped drop shadows out of the photos to make this approach work.

Overall, the brochure feels as deluxe as the furniture inside, but it's still affordable enough to be feasible as a retail giveaway. The thick, coated stock gives the piece a substantial, upscale feel. It's also sturdy enough that the brochure can stand up on its own, creating something akin to a shrunken trade-show display. It's seductive enough to make a design lover splurge on some new living room furniture.

▼ *Since the design team wrote the brochure's copy, they had the luxury of cutting words to match the available space, even tweaking the text for good line breaks.*

Knoll has always designed furnishings that inspire, evolve and endure. More than 30 of our classic designs are included in the permanent collection of MoMA, and our signature pieces number many more. This design leadership defines the past and future of Knoll, and we're adding new elements to our collection of modern classics every year.

Womb
Chair
Eero
Saarinen

With Knoll Space, Knoll has assembled the best of its past and present for the home and home office.

PaperClip®
Table
Vignelli
Design

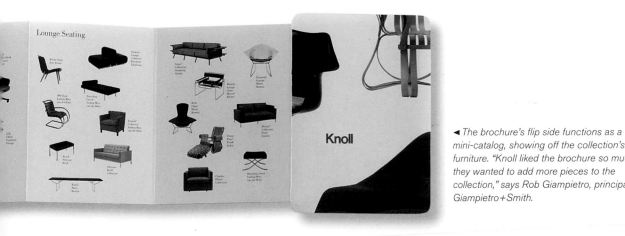

Lounge Seating

Knoll

◄ *The brochure's flip side functions as a mini-catalog, showing off the collection's furniture. "Knoll liked the brochure so much they wanted to add more pieces to the collection," says Rob Giampietro, principal of Giampietro+Smith.*

THE CLIENT: NEENAH PAPER

DESIGN FIRM: AND PARTNERS

Neenah Paper

WHAT'S YOUR COLOR?

▼ *And Partners created this book, which focuses on color and personality, as a promotion for Neenah Paper. The firm chose to use both a clear foil and embossing to help the N and speech bubble stand out on the cover. Inside the piece, the gatefold hides the back of the embossing and makes the perfect spot for the table of contents.*

"I'm a blue orange brown," says David Schimmel, president and creative director of And Partners in New York City. He talks about this three-color designation in the same lighthearted way you might discuss your horoscope, pointing out the personality traits—visionary and dreamer—associated with his color preferences. No, he hasn't been drafted into a new age movement geared toward graphic designers.

Schimmel referenced the Dewey Color System, a scientifically valid color-based personality test, as the subject of a small flip book that And Partners designed for Neenah Paper. The Dewey system was developed by Dewey Sadka, a former staffing agency owner, as a way to understand people through color. Think of it as a shorter, visual version of the Myers-Briggs personality test.

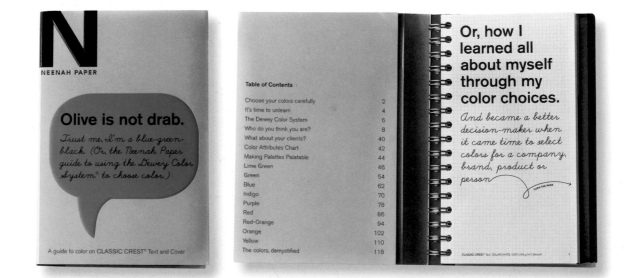

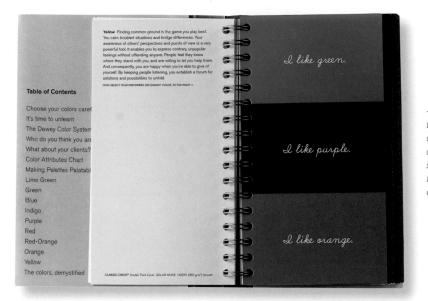

◄ *The beginning of the book leads readers through a simple personality test based on the colors they like most. These three colors—green, purple, and orange—are separated by perforation. This allows users to tear them apart and flip over the appropriate card to learn about their personality.*

As you browse the first few pages of the book, you'll be asked to choose your favorite color within several sets of three colors. Flip over the page or card bearing your preferred shade and you'll uncover a paragraph about your personality traits. Prefer yellow over blue and red? Dewey says, "You calm troubled situations and bridge differences." If you like yellow and purple, you're passionate and open to change. In his own informal poll of test takers, Schimmel found the descriptions to be uncannily accurate.

Neenah tapped And Partners to turn the Dewey system into a resource for the graphic design community—one that would be useful enough to stick around studios and help build the Neenah brand. Since Sadka had already put together several books on his creation, there was a great deal of material to pull from. "It seemed like they wanted everything and the kitchen sink in this book," Schimmel says. "It was very complicated information, and the application was difficult." His firm worked closely with Sadka as they pared down the source material and made it more relevant for designers.

To accomplish the latter, the firm added a section called "What about your clients?" that talks about applying the system's proven color attributes to brands. There's a foldout chart that shows which shades to choose if you're trying to convey stability, impulsiveness, or a host of other descriptors. It takes something subjective and makes it objective—a handy tool for any client meeting. The bulk of the book consists of foldout color palettes based on different base colors—a resource that a designer could put to use on almost any project. There are about 1,300 different colors in the book, and tabs labeled with the base color names make this guide easy to navigate.

By selecting colors and considering their attributes, you enhance the opportunity for your message to be appropriately received.

Now, when you present color to your clients you can inform them that your choices are based on colors that have proven responses — not just your gut instinct or personal aesthetic — that can help better position their brands.

◄ This color attributes chart folds out to help designers put the Dewey Color System to use. Creatives can scan down the sides of the chart to find the message they're trying to convey in a given project and then move across the chart to match the quality with the appropriate color(s).

The piece took close to nine months to complete, and as a result of this effort, it's highly usable. The designers chose a spiral wire binding for its practicality. This feature makes the book easier to use because it always lies flat as you go through the pages. Plus, the double-sided palette sheets are accordion-folded, so they can be pulled out to more than twice the book's width when in use. "This enables you to look at things side-by-side and play with them," Schimmel says. "If you go with these color palettes, you're not going to have what Sadka calls a 'color oops.'"

Another big challenge was recreating all the colors within the Dewey system; they're built colors rather than Pantone color formulas. "Once we got the design and concept worked out, we had to figure out the prototypes of the colors," Schimmel says. His firm went back and forth with a number of press proofs to get them just right. Then they included the six-color process formats for many of the colors in the back of the book.

The piece also promotes Neenah's Classic Crest paper and demonstrates how well solid colors print on this uncoated paper. Pages of vibrant red and blue make better testimonials than any copy. This book also helps position Neenah, in conjunction with Sadka, as a color expert and provides ongoing value for designers. "People seem to love it," Schimmel says.

▲ A clever accordion fold means that palettes rest comfortably in the book until a designer unfolds them to compare color options. This approach allows for side-by-side color comparisons.

The colors, demystified.

Six-color process format (c/m/y/k/o/g)

▲ To make the book easier to use, the design team included color builds for key shades in the back of the book. Humorous, friendly headlines make the content more inviting and simpler to absorb.

THE CLIENT: UNIVERSITY OF FLORIDA SCHOOL OF ART AND ART HISTORY

DESIGN FIRM: CONNIE HWANG DESIGN

University of Florida School of Art and Art History

CREATIVE FOLDING

Connie Hwang needed to figure out how to make the promotional brochure for the Workshop for Art Research and Practice (WARP) at the University of Florida School of Art and Art History stand out despite a relatively modest budget. The piece's ultimate form emerged from a two-hour meeting with the client and an oversized sheet of paper. "We just sat there folding and folding," says Hwang, principal of Connie Hwang Design and an assistant professor of graphic design at the Gainesville-based university. "We wanted something that could stand up."

◄ A unique fold created from a rectangular sheet allows this brochure to stand up. This feature helps the piece attract the attention of young high school and college students.

▲ *Besides allowing the piece to stand up, these two triangles represent the couple that teaches this art program.*

The piece needed to be eye-catching enough to attract the target audience of both high school seniors and current art students. And the client wanted the brochure to function as a template, so they could update the images with new student work. Hwang's solution is both simple and elegant. She folded the rectangular sheet in half to form a square, then folded the square on the diagonal to create a standing triangle. This process results in a form you immediately want to pick up and unfold to see exactly how it works.

The two triangles that allow the piece to stand up also reference WARP, which is taught by a couple. "You can't have one without the other," Hwang says. WARP, which is geared to freshmen, includes both classroom and studio instruction and encompasses everything from creative process to artistic integrity. It also covers a wide range of disciplines.

The brochure's cover uses the school's standard color palette, and the first spread gives a brief overview of the program. When the piece is completely unfolded, it features a range of student work intercepted by diagonal lines. Hwang started with roughly 200 images from the client. "We just found the most interesting ones that represented all the disciplines within the school," she says. These can be swapped out easily when the piece is updated. And the diagonal lines? They're a nod to the program's interdisciplinary research.

To make sure this unusual format would actually work, a fair amount of testing took place. Hwang mailed a blank version to make sure it wouldn't get mangled by the post office and worked hard to select the right paper—some stocks crack when folded. Additionally, Hwang ran her idea by the printer to make sure the unusual folds were possible.

► *This spread's design makes it easy for the program to update the brochure with new student projects for future printings.*

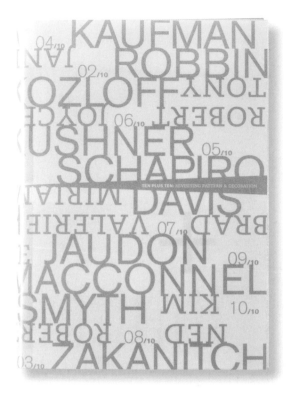

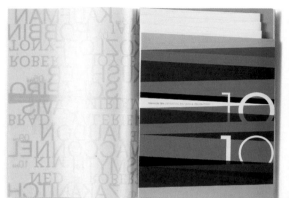

▲ *This exhibition catalog comes wrapped in a vellum cover with a metallic finish. The text is printed in metallic ink and features the artists' names in a pleasing pattern. Both elements are a nod to the metallic elements within many of the show's paintings.*

Hwang also incorporated folding into a small catalog she created for an exhibit at the University Gallery. The show, *Ten Plus Ten: Revisiting Pattern & Decoration,* featured works by 10 artists prominent in the pattern and decoration movement of the 1970s. There were two pieces in the show from each artist—one from the 1970s and one that was created fairly recently. Hwang wanted to reflect the show's key concepts—pattern and decoration—through the tools of graphic design.

"When I was brainstorming, the client said, 'Just take an image and put it on the cover,'" she says. "But the work is so diverse, it's really hard to pick one. I decided to create my own pattern." On the brochure's vellum jacket, Hwang uses typography as a pattern, while still keeping the names of all ten artists readable. For the actual brochure cover, she created a pattern inspired by the colors from the 1970s-era pieces within the exhibition.

In fact, many of Hwang's design decisions were driven by the desire to represent both pattern and decoration within the piece. The accordion fold—inspired by a piece in the exhibit painted on a Japanese screen door—creates its own pattern, while the numbers and lines embossed on the cover fall under decoration. "When I design, I really try to include all the traditional printing techniques I can to reinforce the concept," she says.

▲ This brochure is constructed from an accordion fold, but since the paper gradually gets higher from the front to the back, the tops of the folded pages create an interesting overlap.

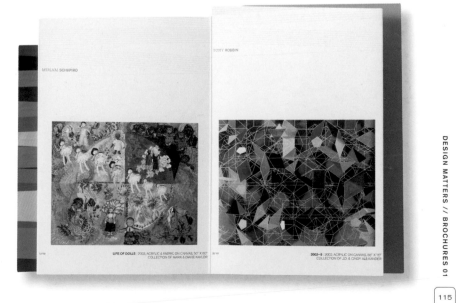

▶ Individual spreads show off artwork from the show, while subtle lines at the top of the page reinforce the idea of pattern and decoration—key themes of the exhibition.

THE CLIENT: DAYCORP PROPERTY DEVELOPMENT AND
THE UNIVERSITY OF ADELAIDE

DESIGN FIRM: VOICE

Daycorp Property Development and the University of Adelaide

DIY TYPE

Though Daycorp Property Development has been around for 30 years, the company only recently started to develop a brand presence. A few years ago, they turned to design firm Voice in Adelaide, Australia, to create a new identity and, more recently, tapped the design firm to create a capabilities brochure. "When this document came up, we wanted to create a visual identity for the book through the type," says Anthony Deleo, a director at Voice.

The firm had created custom characters for Daycorp's logo and decided to expand them into a full set for this brochure. "We wanted to make sure the typeface felt strong and felt like it belonged to a big industry," says Scott Carslake, a director at Voice. Since the typeface is quite structural, it helps Daycorp project confidence—a quality that helps them partner with other companies on large developments. This typeface, simply referred to as Daycorp, appears in headlines and display copy throughout the piece, creating both compelling shapes and a strong visual thread.

▼ *Designers at Voice created the custom typeface that dominates this cover to help the client carve out a brand identity. The copy wraps from the front of the brochure around the spine to the back.*

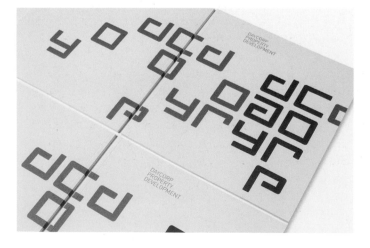

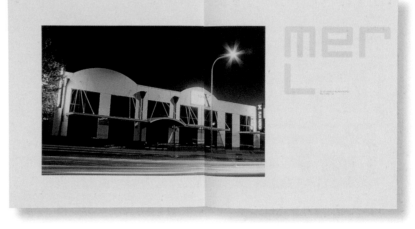

◄ *The Daycorp custom typeface dominates section dividers, giving readers a strong visual cue that they're about to look at a different category of projects. Text blocks are set in an off-the-shelf typeface called Interstate.*

► *Since the projects featured in this brochure aren't all naturally beautiful, designers hired a fine art photographer, rather than an architectural one, to help capture each location in its best light. "He brought a lot to the table," says Anthony Deleo, a director at the design firm Voice.*

In addition to building brand awareness, this piece needed to highlight some of Daycorp's projects—a task that wasn't as easy as it sounds. "We knew some of their sites weren't very attractive," Deleo says. "We really had to sit down and figure out how to approach the photography." To help solve this problem, the designers hired a fine art photographer rather than an architectural one. Digital shots came first, and then the team brainstormed about how best to capture each site. What time of day? Which angle works best? Does it need people or movement? The photographer was an integral part of this process.

Overall, this brochure has a simple, elegant feel. It's an approach that starts things off on the right foot for Daycorp, which had never created a sophisticated print piece before. The layouts are uncluttered and let the emphasis fall on the photography and display type. One or two images on most spreads, along with ample white space, allow Daycorp's work to stand out. The piece definitely takes a big step toward establishing a visual identity for the developer.

► To make this piece compelling within a limited budget, designers created handwritten notes on many of the photos. These teasers help draw people into the main copy by quickly telling stories.

Voice also created custom typography for a fundraising brochure designed for the University of Adelaide, although it was somewhat less formal. In addition to traditional type, there are short, handwritten notes and doodles scrawled across the piece's full-page photos. And these casual elements play a key role in the brochure's concept. "It's a way of making people aware there's a different message on the page," Deleo says.

The brochure hinges on the stories of amazing people connected with the university, including both individuals who donate money and those who benefit from those funds. There's a ninety-three-year-old who earned her masters in anthropology and a young woman who researches Alzheimer's disease using zebra fish. Carslake's hand-penned notes quickly highlight each person's story and help forge an emotional connection with readers. This helps to draw people into the main text to learn more about these extraordinary people and various fundraising efforts.

To create the handwritten text, Carslake printed out each photograph on laser paper and put it on a light box. He laid another piece of paper over the top and started handwriting the type. Once he was satisfied, he scanned his creation into the computer. "It was a very low-budget job," he says. "We had to find ways to make it interesting."

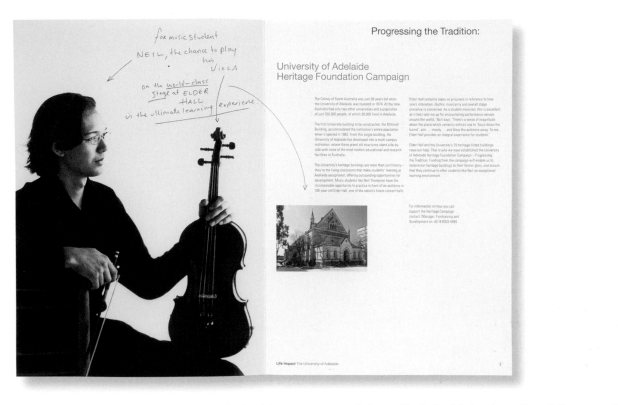

▲ To make the brochure engaging, the design team put the focus on people who participate in and benefit from the university's fundraising efforts. This approach helps forge a strong emotional connection with readers.

Each of the portraits was shot specifically for this brochure, though there wasn't enough room in the budget for styling. The subjects just showed up at the shoot in their own clothes and were photographed without much fuss over their appearance. Since most of the university's brochures are quite colorful, designers decided to lower the saturation of the photographs to differentiate the piece. This approach also gave the brochure a softer feel.

► Many of the university's printed materials use photos from a preexisting photography bank, so designers shot the oversized portraits featured in this brochure to help set the piece apart. Smaller images were pulled from existing imagery.

THE CLIENT: ARENT FOX

DESIGN FIRM: DESIGN ARMY

Arent Fox

SELLING GOOD IDEAS

"It's not about B.S.—it's about telling the truth. I tell the client, 'I'm in this with you. If you fail, I fail.'"

—Pum Lefebure, creative director at Design Army

Law firm brochures tend to be a little too starched around the collar—in fact, you can probably describe the typical formula. Two men wearing suits and shaking hands. A buttoned-up layout and muted color palette. It's all a little too predictable. So when the team at Design Army revamped Arent Fox's brochures, they wanted to avoid the visual equivalent of legalese.

To help this law firm stand out from the competition, the Washington, D.C.–based design shop decided to run with the client's tagline: "Smart in your world." This brief phrase helped inspire the concept for a capabilities brochure. Rather than emphasize a client list and case wins, the piece focuses on the people and stories that make the firm unique. You can read about an unusual lawsuit against building owners whose tenants sell fake Louis Vuitton bags or learn about a racial discrimination settlement with the Library of Congress. They're the kinds of tales you'd find more readily in a magazine or newspaper than a piece of marketing collateral.

To enrich these stories, all the copy is presented in a narrative style and paired with original location photography. The firm's lawyers come across as warm and intelligent, the kind of folks you might like to invite over for dinner. In addition, Design Army made the piece friendly, with a clean layout and liberal use of blue and red—two of the firm's brand colors. The third color, gray, serves as a complement throughout the book. There's also another important way the brochure makes its mark: instead of a typical 8½ x 11–inch (21.6 x 27.9–cm) or 9 x 12–inch (22.9 x 30.5–cm) piece, it measures an intimate 5½ x 7½ inches (14 x 17.8 cm).

◄ This capabilities piece stands out from other law-firm brochures with a friendly, engaging design and strong storytelling. "If you sit in the middle of the road, it's a scary place to be," says Pum Lefebure, a creative director at Design Army. "You get run over."

Sounds like the perfect solution, right? But it didn't come to fruition without its fair share of obstacles. Creative director Pum Lefebure spent a lot of time on the phone with Arent Fox's chief marketing officer, giving her the rationale behind concepts and design decisions. Those conversations sometimes stretched as long as an hour, but they provided crucial information for selling ideas to the law firm's fifteen partners. "It's not about B.S.," says Lefebure. "It's about telling the truth. I tell the client, 'I'm in this with you. If you fail, I fail.'" This allows her to stand up for ideas without becoming an adversary—and since the firm doesn't have account executives, the creative staff is able to present the thinking behind their work with genuine passion.

► Each case study in the book starts with an engaging, first-person lead-in. This copy is presented on a page flooded with a solid color to signal a new story to readers.

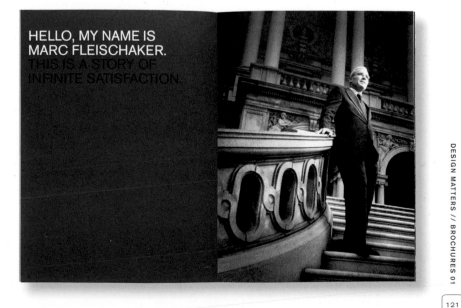

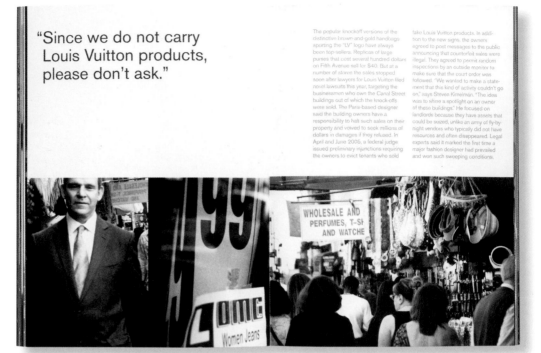

"Since we do not carry Louis Vuitton products, please don't ask."

The popular knockoff versions of the distinctive brown-and-gold handbags sporting the "LV" logo have always been top-sellers. Replicas of large purses that cost several hundred dollars on Fifth Avenue sell for $40. But at a number of stores the sales stopped soon after lawyers for Louis Vuitton filed novel lawsuits this year, targeting the businessmen who own the Canal Street buildings out of which the knock-offs were sold. The Paris-based designer said the building owners have a responsibility to halt such sales on their property and vowed to seek millions of dollars in damages if they refused. In April and June 2005, a federal judge issued preliminary injunctions requiring the owners to evict tenants who sold fake Louis Vuitton products. In addition to the new signs, the owners agreed to post messages to the public announcing that counterfeit sales were illegal. They agreed to permit random inspections by an outside monitor to make sure that the court order was followed. "We wanted to make a statement that this kind of activity couldn't go on," says Steven Kimelman. "The idea was to shine a spotlight on an owner of these buildings." He focused on landlords because they have assets that could be seized, unlike an army of fly-by-night vendors who typically did not have resources and often disappeared. Legal experts said it marked the first time a major fashion designer had prevailed and won such sweeping conditions.

▲ *Original location photography helps convey the individual stories within this brochure. It also sets the piece apart from other law-firm efforts, bypassing the obligatory shots of businessmen shaking hands in an office. The brochure was a big hit with clients and helped seal the deal with candidates during the firm's hiring process.*

The Design Army team also pays close attention to all the details as they execute projects. Arent Fox's capabilities brochure, for example, comes in a red sleeve with a blind emboss on the cover. "It feels special," says Lefebure. "It's like a coffee table book rather than something you put on your shelf." She also played an integral role in making the book's photography seem so natural, chatting with the lawyers during the four-day shoot to help them relax. Plus, the team came up with an innovative solution to accommodate the piece's two different audiences. A letter from the firm's chairman was included in brochures handed out at the company's annual meeting, but since it was printed on vellum, it was easy to remove from the version sent to Fortune 500 companies.

In addition to this brochure, Design Army created a colorful, friendly piece to help the law firm recruit summer associates from top law schools. AF101 takes a form familiar to students: a spiral notebook. Pages flip up to reveal custom illustrations created by the design firm, while text highlights the work and social opportunities that the aspiring lawyers will enjoy. A colorful sushi illustration, for example, represents diversity, while a subway map reinforces the firm's practice areas and the idea of summer in the city. There's also a blank page for notes and a pocket in the back where students can tuck additional information.

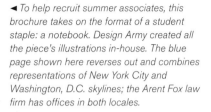

◄ To help recruit summer associates, this brochure takes on the format of a student staple: a notebook. Design Army created all the piece's illustrations in-house. The blue page shown here reverses out and combines representations of New York City and Washington, D.C. skylines; the Arent Fox law firm has offices in both locales.

The piece worked so well that the law firm reprinted it for another recruiting season. Since the design is fresh and modern, Lefebure predicts it could work for several years. She tells her clients that if they take the time to do something the right way, there's no reason it can't last. "Our design is not about being trendy," she says. Instead, it's about being clear and intelligent as you work to get across the right message, which is a definite step up from the conventions found in most law-firm brochures.

THE CLIENT: OFSET YAPIMEVI

DESIGN FIRM: ESEN KAROL

Ofset Yapimevi

STRENGTH IN NUMBERS

After walking down a few aisles at a trade show, all the printed materials start to run together into a faceless sea of information. People try to hand you brochures and business cards as your bag begins to sag under the weight. It doesn't take long to become choosy about what you're willing to cart home—a fact that makes it all the more important for brochures to send an immediate and compelling message.

◄► *This brochure for printer Ofset Yapimevi comes in a thin paper sleeve. The outer cover features the company's brand colors and a series of numbers. The latter are used to tell the printer's story, revealing everything from the total years of experience held by the company's employees (1,000) to the average number of projects completed annually (4,500).*

Designer Esen Karol knew she was up against this tough scenario when printer Ofset Yapimevi tapped her to design the company's first promotional brochure. Though the printer already had a great reputation among designers, the company wanted to expand its reach to other audiences and catch the eye of European businesses. They needed a printed piece to hand out at major trade shows such as the Frankfort Book Fair and take on sales calls. The goal was to create something light and small that would stand out among standard-issue brochures from big corporations.

This sizable challenge, however, didn't come with a big budget, so Karol, based in Istanbul, needed to figure out how to make an impact without pricey bells and whistles. The solution was a strong, slightly offbeat concept that told the printer's story through a series of numbers. Rather than feature the kind of running text you might find on any given printer's website, Karol put together a series of questions for her client that could only be answered with numbers. The resulting figures provide all the company's key selling points in a format that's both intellectually and visually compelling.

If you take a close look at the page that starts with 10,700, for example, you'll realize that it represents the number of CDs in Ofset Yapimevi's archives. That's good news if you want to reprint something from two years ago and can't quite put your hands on the files. Another panel highlights an equally important detail: there are 168 hours in the Turkish printer's workweek. This point sets the company apart from European printers, which can't run at night due to regulations. Other panels feature everything from the number of languages that company employees speak to how many sheets of paper they print in twenty-four hours.

▲ *To emphasize that the information on each card can stand alone, the folds are perforated. This means that readers can rip them apart if they choose—perhaps hanging a favorite image up on the bulletin board.*

In addition to drawing readers into the piece, this approach gave Karol a powerful graphic hook. The numbers essentially become headlines and provide a bold, typographic element on each page. This concept also served as a clever workaround for a budget that didn't have room for a copywriter. Since Karol needed to write the text herself, she had to pick a style that wouldn't look amateurish when executed by a designer.

Karol put this same DIY ethic into play when it came to the photography. Again, financial constraints didn't allow her to commission original photography, so she picked up a camera and spent a day at the printer. Since most factories are bright and look quite similar, she decided to focus on the details. She took as many shots as she could in a single day, then sorted through her efforts to see which images might work.

Though they're not meant to be perfect images, the photographs still accomplish something important: They set a warm and intimate mood for the piece. Since the close-up shots are darker than a typical office or factory setting, they make the piece feel friendly rather than businesslike. Karol's images also take people to such unexpected places as the inside of a cyan ink can. "It puts the reader in a position where they wouldn't be normally," she says. "You don't stand behind the boss and see what he's writing."

The accordion fold perfectly pulls together all of the brochure's elements, while the small size makes it easy to stick in your pocket and carry it to a meeting. "It's like a big business card," Karol says. And the individual panels reinforce the fact that each piece of information stands on its own. There's no true end or beginning to the piece because there isn't any hierarchy of information. Each panel tells a snippet of the story and is separated by perforated folds. "The perforation emphasizes that those are individual fragments," Karol says. "Even alone, they mean something."

The piece's format also means that readers can interact with it in different ways. "You can read it like a book and you can put it on a table like an object," says Karol. Or if you fall in love with a particular photograph, you can tear off the panel and hang it on your bulletin board. The piece is printed on thick stock, so it stands easily on a desk or holds up well if someone decides to hang it on the wall.

A sleeve featuring the printer's corporate colors holds the piece together. It's meant to be torn off like a present, but many people slide it carefully out of the sleeve. The tight fit, however, means that once it's out of the sleeve, the brochure can't be slid back inside. "When you give it to someone, it is obvious it's not been touched before," Karol says. This makes reading the piece a special experience. As Karol puts it, the piece was produced inexpensively, but it certainly doesn't look or feel as if it was done on a budget. Instead, it accomplishes everything it should in an effortless way.

▲◄ *Though designer Esen Karol wanted readers to rip this outer cover off the brochure like wrapping paper, many people chose to slide the brochure out without harming the sleeve. Either way, readers know they're the first person to lay hands on the piece because it doesn't slide back into the tight-fitting cover.*

THE CLIENT: AMERICAN RED CROSS

DESIGN FIRM: FLAT

American Red Cross

A DELICATE SUBJECT

There's been no shortage of words and imagery remembering the emotional landscape surrounding 9/11. But as the tragedy's five-year anniversary approached, the American Red Cross wanted to document their relief efforts. It's a complex story, so the organization hired New York design firm Flat to help chronicle the disaster response with a website and print piece.

When the project started, the nonprofit handed Flat a pile of numbers and a detailed timeline, so the design team spent the first few months simply trying to understand the content. How should it be presented? What was the best way to communicate all these details? At least one thing became clear fairly quickly. "What was important to us was to not fall into the cliché visualization of 9/11," says Petter Ringbom, a partner at Flat. "We didn't want to do dark imagery. We wanted to treat it differently. Respectfully."

► *For the five-year anniversary of 9/11, the American Red Cross hired New York design firm Flat to create a brochure and website chronicling the organization's relief efforts. This piece was printed on relatively modest stock because the organization didn't want to send the message that they were spending a lot of money on the brochure.*

The design team needed to figure out how to express the gravity of the response effort without resorting to tragic photos. Luckily, the Red Cross kept an archive of objects from their five-year relief effort, and these items showed the emotional side of the organization's work without needlessly pushing people's buttons. The collection included everything from a hazmat suit to children's drawings, and the firm had these artifacts photographed against a white background without drop shadows or other distractions.

Perhaps this straightforward approach wields the most power on the brochure's cover, which features a folded American flag set against a stark white background. There isn't a title or logo to distract from the image's impact. "This is one of the few projects where you can use an American flag on the cover without feeling gross about it," Ringbom says. This particular flag also holds special significance because it once flew on top of the federal building in Oklahoma City that was bombed in 1995.

▲► *To make the brochure more accessible to readers, Flat spread the substantial amount of copy out over forty-some pages. This approach gave the text plenty of room to breathe and allowed the firm to draw people into the piece with compelling artwork.*

Ringbom believes that the simple geometric form makes a humble statement, one much different than the tone set by an American flag flying in the wind. It also creates a subtle arrow that invites readers to open the piece and start exploring the information inside. The client, however, wasn't immediately sold on the idea. "They were a little hesitant about having a cover with nothing else on it but the American flag," Ringbom says. But since the image felt so strong by itself, the design team convinced them that it was a sound approach. The organization's logo, along with the brochure's title, appears on the back cover.

This engaging approach also serves another important purpose: it helps the brochure stand out when it lands on the desks of members of congress. Since this elite audience is inundated with materials, many poorly designed, this thoughtful approach increases the odds that this brochure will stand out. In addition to these key decision makers, the brochure's target audience includes Red Cross staff, clients, and volunteers—all people with a real stake in the relief efforts.

This brochure's interior design works hard to make dense information friendlier and more accessible. Though the Red Cross provided the copy, the design team made the decision to stretch it out over roughly forty pages. This gives the text plenty of room to breathe and makes it less intimidating for potential readers. There's plenty of white space and artwork to balance out the text and section dividers give the viewer's eyes a place to rest with blank pages that feature single-word descriptors. The liberal use of pull quotes and subheads provides additional points of entry to draw readers into the main text.

The piece balances financial facts and program details with the human side of the Red Cross effort. In addition to all those object images, a fair number of spreads feature friendly, smiling faces—everyone from volunteers to clients—who were interviewed for the website. When these videos were shot, the firm took the opportunity also to take simple portraits. The resulting images, which are paired with short quotes, take the piece from the abstract to the individual, an approach that makes the overall message much more salient.

At its core, this brochure accomplishes an important goal for the Red Cross: transparency. The months after 9/11 came with a major shift for the organization, in which the funds donated for this tragedy were spent only on this tragedy. In the past, the nonprofit allocated prioritized funds across all its efforts. It also provided a fitting ending to a five-year-long relief program, one that ended around the same time this piece came out. "This was not about raising money," Ringbom says. "The real goal was to show people what the Red Cross had done."

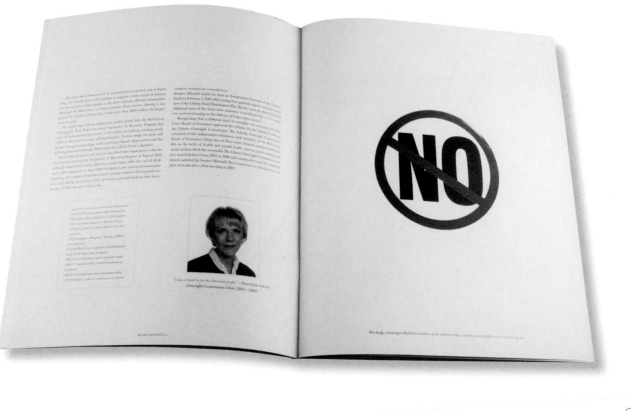

THE CLIENT: THE CHILENO BAY CLUB

DESIGN FIRM: FINE DESIGN GROUP

The Chileno Bay Club

SELLING PARADISE

It doesn't sound like a tough problem on the surface: design marketing materials for a slice of beachfront paradise in Mexico. But when the Chileno Bay Club hired FINE Design Group, they brought along an interesting set of challenges. This private community's villas and estates don't yet actually exist. And since they're quite pricey, there's only a small demographic with the means to buy. It put the design team in the middle of a delicate puzzle. How could they make people fall in love with a vision not yet fully realized? "We had to sell an aspirational fantasy," says Kenn Fine, creative director at the San Francisco firm.

◄ *This sales brochure promotes The Chileno Bay Club, an upscale vacation community yet to be built. To help potential buyers get a sense for the place, the team at FINE Design Group combined lifestyle photography with watercolor illustrations to create a travel journal feel.*

So the design team set about familiarizing themselves with the dreams and ideas behind Chileno Bay. They took the time to meet with all the key players working on the development—everyone from the architects to the golf course designer. The design firm also made a pilgrimage to the land where this luxury community would eventually sprout, gaining first-hand knowledge of Los Cabos, Mexico. "It really gave us a sense of place," Fine says. "There are some places on the planet that just have this feel about them."

From there, the firm worked collaboratively with the client to define the target audience for this sales brochure and related marketing collateral. They tapped both research and creative intuition to paint a picture of the people who were likely to buy a second or third home at Chileno Bay. This process covered everything from age, income, and lifestyle to relationships with other brands. By the time this phase concluded, the design team knew exactly who the development's print materials needed to reach: a wealthy, older crowd with children who were about to, or had already, left home. These were people looking for a getaway spot where they could bring together their whole families.

◄► The piece comes in an envelope with an intricate pattern laser cut into the cover. This creates a look and feel similar to the elaborate ironwork typical of Spanish architecture, the predominant style for the community.

They were also the individuals who would eventually shape the personality of the Chileno Bay Club. To capture their attention and communicate the development's key traits, the sales brochure needed to exude quality, richness and exclusivity. One way the firm accomplished this was by going beyond the conventions used in materials for other properties, which tend to mix large imagery with flowery type. FINE took things past good looks by developing a concept that highlighted the exceptional experience offered at Chileno Bay. "It's meant to have a dash of this travel journal feel," Fine says.

The piece looks like an elegant artist's scrapbook, one that lets you know that a week spent at the development would be something to write home about. It mixes original watercolor illustrations, which convey the poetry of the ocean and wildlife, with gorgeous lifestyle photography. The latter are often presented with white borders to resemble old-fashioned snapshots, creating a seductive combination, inviting readers to imagine painting on the beach or enjoying a picnic with their children. It also gets across the message that the Chileno Bay Club is a step above other vacation home options.

Since the photography plays a key role in bringing the atmosphere of the eventual development alive, the design team invested the time and money necessary for an on-site shoot in Mexico. They hired models, stylists, and wardrobe people to help pull together just the right vibe. Overall, the goal was to create a stylistic impression of Chileno Bay through lifestyle imagery. Potential buyers need to be able to see themselves in the brochure and start daydreaming about spending time in this vacation community.

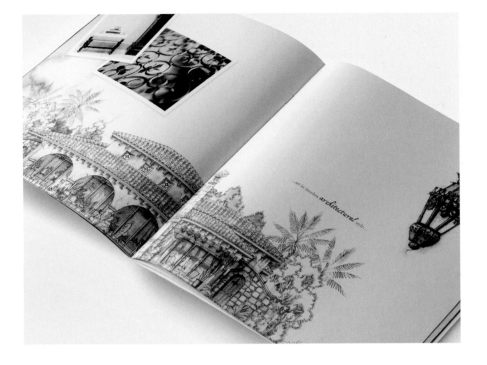

FINE, however, didn't follow a typical photo shoot formula. "We have a unique approach to photography," he says. "We don't do staging the way most people do." For example, rather than manufacture a party scene, the team simply threw a party and captured photos as it was happening. They gave minor direction as things progressed, such as asking models to smile or walk in a certain direction, but they didn't stage single scenes over and over. This approach worked especially well for shots with children, who have a difficult time looking natural when they're asked to repeat actions or poses.

All these idyllic images emerge from an envelope that gives the brochure an even better chance of carving out time in a recipient's busy day. The piece comes in a brown envelope with an intricate pattern laser cut from the cover. Although the studio created this repeating design, it took its cues from the development's Spanish architecture, mimicking the complex patterns found within its iron gates. In essence, the envelope forms an elaborate entry gate to the brochure, reinforcing the idea of exclusivity.

It took some time and thought, however, to execute the laser cut properly. The pattern had to be revised a few times because cutting away too much paper was making the piece fall apart. Laser cutting can also leave burn marks on one side of the stock—much like a burnt marshmallow. Stock in dark colors helps hide these blemishes—and, in this case, any marks appear on the inside of the envelope, where they won't be seen. This exquisitely cut pattern, however, is sure to lure recipients to open the envelope and explore the brochure inside.

DESIGN MATTERS // BROCHURES 01

135

THE CLIENT: UPPERCUT IMAGES

DESIGN FIRM: PLANET PROPAGANDA

UpperCut Images

THE STOCK MARKET

▼ *"It needed to be a piece that would showcase the photography and feel higher-end than a regular stock book," says Travis Cain, senior designer at Planet Propaganda, about this launch brochure for UpperCut Images. To run the photography unencumbered by type, he split the launch brochure in two by gluing a small text brochure on the cover of the larger image book. "This was targeted at designers who, quite honestly, might not read all this copy," he says.*

There's a short, catchy phrase on the cover of UpperCut's launch brochure that sums things up best: "Stock that isn't." These three little words tell you everything you need to know about this new stock agency, and they're also how the company plans to stand out in a crowded market—with smart, artistic images from top photographers. Since the photos aren't boring or clichéd, the agency's marketing materials couldn't be either.

When Planet Propaganda started working on this new brand, they came up with the "Stock that isn't" tagline to concisely communicate this newcomer's approach. From there, the Madison, Wisconsin, design team used this mantra as a driving force in much of the stock agency's print collateral. The launch brochure, for example, not only starts with this phrase but also backs up the implied promise with the photography inside.

▲ *When pairing images on a spread, Cain looked for common threads in composition, color, content, or feel. As shown here, the knight and white horse seem like a natural fit, while the goat and feet share a similar composition.*

Flip through the pages and you'll discover everything from a woman in business attire lying at the bottom of a staircase to brown, furry rabbit ears popping out from the slots in a retro toaster. "I like images with a bigger implied narrative," says senior designer Travis Cain. "Even if you aren't sure exactly what's going on." He looked for photos with a sense of mystery or intrigue, the ones most likely to capture the attention of image-weary graphic designers and art buyers.

Cain also made another crucial decision to curry favor with his target audience. He created two separate brochures, effectively quarantining the text from the photos. A smaller 8 x 10–inch (20.3 x 25.4–cm) brochure provides all the sales points while a larger 9½ x 13–inch (22.9 x 33–cm) piece features large, uninterrupted images on white paper. To combine the two, he glued the smaller piece to the front of its big brother. "Many designers skip the copy anyway," Cain says. "But they can still find it if they want to learn more."

During this piece's creation, UpperCut was still launching, so Cain worked closely with the company to choose images. The client sent choices his way, and he had access to raw images on the company's server. He searched for photos that presented subject matter in fresh, interesting ways and made a point to showcase work from top photographers, whose names helped boost the agency's artistic street cred. His overall goal? Show images with strong art direction and little or no stock-like aftertaste.

Some selections dominate full spreads whereas others become friendly neighbors. When pairing photos, Cain tried to find a visual connection in content, composition, color, or feel. A picture of a white horse, for example, makes perfect sense across from a knight outfitted in a full suit of armor. Other images are united by the dominance of water or a common focus on a beautiful woman. Cain wanted to present the kind of artistic, aspirational images many designers wish they could use more often.

DAVID MAISEL vs. Powerless

SEAN KENNEDY SANTOS vs. Spoonfed

▲ ► *This small book promotes top photographers in UpperCut's stable and its unusual format creates two brochures in one. Each cover—and the pages that follow— promotes a different photographer. When you encounter the second story in the middle of the book, the pages change direction. It's a signal to look for the other cover and restart the experience.*

For those intrigued enough by the visuals to want to learn more, the text brochure cycles through a range of warm colors from UpperCut's brand palette. Each spread features three levels of copy: a brief topic on the left-hand page, followed by a catchy headline on the other side, and a little explanatory copy below. This layout makes it easy for designers to skim right to the things they most want to know. For example, fairly large copy reading "Rights Protection" lives across the way from this catchy headline: "Creative license meets creative licensing." A little farther down the page, additional copy explains the ins and outs of rights-managed stock and rights protection.

This launch brochure effectively makes the case for UpperCut's philosophy and photography, but it doesn't spend much time focusing on the people behind the lens. "We really wanted to do a printed piece that would promote the art of the photographer," Cain says. The idea was to give designers a glimpse into the thought processes of top photographers from the agency's stable. This strategy also reinforces a key brand message—that these images are a cut above the offerings from competing stock companies.

"I always remembered that body language of putting your hands on your hips means *I know everything.* And I thought: *This guy does.* I've seen how hard he works...that guy deserves to put his hands on his hips."

"Let's concentrate on the emotion of the shot, draw on t

Casually known as the shooter booklet, this horizontal piece packs two brochures into one. Each cover and the subsequent pages promote a different photographer—and in the middle of the book, the pages literally change direction. Imagine two books stuck together with one upside down. This format gave equal prominence to each of the two photographers, Sean Kennedy Santos and David Maisel.

Inside the book, each photographer's photos are integrated with quotes about his creativity and working philosophy. "We tried to match up what he was saying with what was going on in a specific image," Cain says. A scene from Italy, for instance, is presented alongside this quote from Maisel: "I could go back to Italy every year and shoot pictures, there's so much there." These kinds of thoughts and insights were culled from videos about the photographers that were created for the UpperCut website and, in Maisel's case, a phone interview with the design firm's copywriter. These behind-the-scenes snippets also add depth and context to the breathtaking imagery, reinforcing the idea that UpperCut's images are about art rather than generic beauty.

▲▼ *Each photographer submitted both original and repurposed images for the book. Cain collaborated with both UpperCut and the photographers on the edit. As a result, there wasn't much cropping, and Cain had to nix an image he wanted to flip for a particular spread. Together, the team worked to greenlight the most provocative images.*

"Lo and behold the actual sculpture of this foot was being restored so we couldn't have access to it, even to photograph it, so we then set about to find the best possible props people in Rome that could make a facsimile of this famous sculpture for us, and we found some great people who did a phenomenal job and it was probably about 1/5 scale of what you see in the final photo—so it was one of those things where we did have to make a digital concoction later."

"I could go back to Italy every year and shoot pictures, there's so much there."

Legal Aid Foundation of Los Angeles

A LONG-TERM RELATIONSHIP

Let's be honest. Many clients change designers, firms, or agencies often; a fact that makes Deanna Kuhlmann-Leavitt's relationship with the Legal Aid Foundation of Los Angeles (LAFLA) quite remarkable. She's worked on the organization's annual report for sixteen years running. "Legal Aid has been an important constant," says the principal of Kuhlmann Leavitt in St. Louis. The client even followed her through a cross-country move.

When she worked on the first report in 1991, Kuhlmann-Leavitt was twenty-five, single, and two years out of design school. Today, she's married, with two kids and a house, and is the principal of a thriving design business. But nearly as important as these sweeping life changes is that Kuhlmann-Leavitt's relationship with LAFLA has evolved from client to friend and her close ties put her in a unique position to communicate the organization's message. "During the past sixteen years, my team and I have been privileged to learn about the personal stories and then present them in book form to a wider audience," she says. "That experience, year in and year out, has forged an emotional connection between me and this great organization."

This intimacy with the organization's personality helps her create annual reports with power and authenticity. As in previous years, this report features the stories of real people served by the organization's lawyers, many of them heartrending tales about individuals trying to climb out of poverty. "We endeavor to capture the reader's attention by presenting the client stories in a way that reveals their determination and dignity," Kuhlmann-Leavitt says. After all, these aren't fictional marketing blurbs, so each individual's story needs to be treated with respect.

▲ *The design team at Kuhlmann Leavitt chose a bold color palette for this brochure, an annual report for the Legal Aid Foundation of Los Angeles. "We wanted the piece to be dramatic without being dark," says Deanna Kuhlmann-Leavitt, the firm's principal. "We want this to be an optimistic story. Not doom and gloom." Red and black make an impact without making the serious but uplifting stories inside feel hopeless.*

Typically, LAFLA's report takes the form of a book, with ample room to chronicle the organization's rich stories. This year, however, LAFLA's new director wanted a piece that could have a longer year-round life and asked for a simple folder that could house different materials throughout the year, thereby making the most of their small marketing budget. The design team at Kuhlman-Leavitt recommended this tall, relatively narrow brochure with a pocket built into the back panel. This format makes the piece versatile enough to promote the organization throughout the year, but it also offers readers a more engaging experience than a typical folder. The inside back pocket houses information that gets updated year-round and, since this is an annual report, it houses the requisite financial data.

The design team didn't waste time setting the tone for the entire piece, splashing a powerful Thomas Jefferson quote across the cover. This commanding statement—"Equal rights for all, special privileges for none"—immediately draws readers into the brochure with a striking red background that emphasizes the boldness of the words. Like all the display type in the brochure, the cover quote is set in Trajan because the stoic face matches the subject matter perfectly. A halo effect behind the quote, which mimics the photos inside, adds another level of interest.

▲ *As the piece unfolds, it reveals the organization's details alongside its clients' stories. This clever pacing captures readers' attention with the emotional story first, so they'll take the time to continue reading to learn more about Legal Aid's structure, efforts, and overall mission.*

Once readers open the piece, they're faced with an engaging spread that chronicles two women's interactions with LAFLA. The design team uses a basic information hierarchy to draw people into the information. Documentary-style photos capture your eye first; then the eye moves to the first sentence of each story, which is reversed out in white and treated much like a pull quote. Those who want to learn more can continue down the page, but the basic story can also be gleaned from the images and display type. The key message from each story, for instance, appears in a few words at the bottom of each page. These compelling phrases include "It's a miracle" and "No one would help."

► *The brochure's back cover features the story of a woman who received assistance from the Legal Aid Foundation of Los Angles. The design team set the all-caps display type in Trajan and the lengthier body copy in Helvetica Light.*

The fact that these personal narratives are placed up front also reflects a well-considered decision about how the piece should unfold. "We feel like if we tell the personal story first, people are more likely to read about the organization and get involved," Kuhlmann-Leavitt says. As readers continue to open up more panels, they're slowly exposed to details about the organization. This informational text appears alongside additional client stories that represent the range of legal areas where LAFLA offers assistance.

Like Kuhlmann-Leavitt, the photographer Everard Williams, Jr. has been involved with LAFLA for sixteen years, absent from only one report along the way. He shot these images in the organization's office and added the spotlight and halo effects after the fact. These subtle touches give the photographs another dimension and keep the focus on the people. "I think it made the piece more powerful," Kuhlman-Leavitt says. Although this often happens over the phone due to budget constraints, one of the firm's designers happened to be in Los Angeles, so he art-directed the shoot in person.

In all, the brochure's content comes across as serious but uplifting. It tells the LAFLA's story in a way that makes you want to take action, whether that's taking the time to read the entire piece or writing out a donation check. All the details and nuances are just right, a feat made easier by the long-lasting ties between client and designer.

Manhattan Theatre Club

A STAR-STUDDED PHOTO SHOOT

When it came time to put together this brochure for the Manhattan Theatre Club (MTC), the design process was the least of the challenges. New York design firm SpotCo became the group's official agency in 2003 and since then has made an effort to reinvent MTC's brochure each year—a strategy meant to increase their subscriber base. For this 2006–2007 piece, the design team worked with photographer Henry Leutwyler to create a series of black-and-white portraits of MTC actors and writers.

Putting together a shoot with a celebrity line-up, however, is a project in its own right. First, MTC's marketing director, Debra Waxman, worked to coordinate the schedules of all the busy participants for a one-day shoot. "Asking the actors and writers to participate is the easy part," she says. "Getting them to commit to a specific date and place while making sure their hair, makeup, and transportation needs are addressed is what gets very complicated." For example, she didn't learn that one of the subjects would be coming to the shoot until fifteen minutes beforehand.

To handle this unexpected turn of events, she tweaked the schedule and let everyone know what was happening. "Communication is essential," she says. "Then no one is surprised or put off when things need to change." SpotCo's photo producer, Mark Rheault, also played a crucial role in making the shoot go seamlessly. He hired and coordinated everyone from stylists to hair and makeup people. "Shooting celebrities can always be a challenge," he says. "You have to enter into it knowing that every subject you shoot needs to feel like they are the only subject being shot that day. No preferential treatment can really be given." This means making sure that hair, makeup, wardrobe, and on-set times are equal for each person.

◄▲ *This Manhattan Theatre Club brochure features gorgeous images of actors and writers. "Henry Leutwyler's black-and-white photography is stunning, and he'd done beautiful work for us on another show," says Gail Anderson, creative director, design, at SpotCo in New York. "We wanted to do an entire season of black-and-white photography for MTC's seven shows, and the season brochure kicked it off."*

Creating the right environment—with everything from music to catering—also makes the whole experience more pleasant. "Mark keeps it all moving and makes sure everyone's taken care of, from the talent to the client," says Gail Anderson, creative director, design. "While one subject is in makeup, another's in wardrobe. Someone's being shot, and another's having lunch. It's a lot to juggle." The day, however, wasn't without some lighter moments. Anderson says she suffered dog envy after meeting Noodle, a Labradoodle that actor Oliver Platt brought with him to the shoot. The photographer took a few shots of the actor and his pet for fun, but these didn't make it into the final piece.

Ultimately, it's these stunning black-and-white photographs that make the brochure so compelling. They're enough to spur a busy professional to pluck this piece out from among the bills and junk that arrive in the mailbox. As readers explore the piece by gradually opening up the barrel roll, they meet more and more of MTC's family members. These actors and writers, with their engaging expressions and poses, are presented on a simple white background. The layout combines these black-and-white images with swaths of red to bold effect. "You really can't go wrong with that palette," Anderson says.

THIS SEASON, TWO OF THE FOUR BEST PLAY TONY AWARD® NOMINEES CAME FROM ONE PLACE: MTC.

WE'RE THRILLED to have been honored with seven 2006 Tony Award nominations, including BEST PLAY for both *Shining City* and *Rabbit Hole*.

ONLY MTC SUBSCRIBERS were guaranteed seats at these winning productions, as well as at our Off-Broadway productions, which this season included *Defiance*, the latest collaboration from the Tony-winning team that brought you *Doubt*.

IN 2006-07, there's even more great theatre awaiting you. We're still putting the finishing touches on our season, but you can be sure that our productions will feature a dazzling array of the theatre's best actors, authors and directors, just like you've come to expect from MTC.

BY BECOMING A SUBSCRIBER TODAY, you'll lock in the very best savings we offer and get early access to the best seats at all three of our stages, both on Broadway and Off.

PLEASE JOIN US AT MTC FOR THE BEST IN THEATRE NEXT SEASON.

SUBSCRIBE TODAY AND SEE *SHINING CITY* AT A SPECIAL PRICE! SEE BACK PANEL FOR MORE DETAILS.

PAUL RUDNICK (Author of next season's *Regrets Only*)
JOHN PATRICK SHANLEY (Author of Tony and Pulitzer Prize-winning sensation *Doubt* and this season's *Defiance*)

Picking the brochure's cover subjects presented another potential challenge. "It's always tricky to call out two or three big names and put everyone else inside," Anderson says. But the team based their choices on two of the most honored shows from MTC's previous season, making Brían F. O'Byrne, Cynthia Nixon, and Oliver Platt the cover trio. Ultimately, Anderson doesn't believe that the participants worry too much about how they're positioned in the final brochure. "They're really all about raising awareness of the organization," she says. "Egos are checked at the door, as rah-rah as that may sound."

In the end, the brochure covers all the bases. It positions MTC as upscale, contemporary, and elegant through the images, layout, and format. Plus, the popular actors on the cover let people know immediately that MTC attracts high-caliber performers—a fact that might make you a little more likely to take out the credit card and become a season subscriber. And since many MTC patrons care as much about the writers as the stars, these prominent scribes are given ample space inside.

As the piece unfolds, it gradually introduces you to actors and writers alongside show and subscription details, the latter typically reversed out of red. This creates the perfect balance between the emotional story and the selling one, giving you the chance to connect for a moment with a favorite playwright or actress as you consider the next season's offerings. Once it's completely unfolded, the piece creates an effect similar to a poster, with ten creative people staring out from a shared space. The combined power of the images are enough to merit hanging the piece up on your bulletin board, where it can serve as temporary artwork or an idea for a future date night.

▲ More of the piece's gorgeous photography reveals itself as readers open up the barrel roll. The elegant layout includes subtle, notched patterns that echo photo borders. "I think we ended up including the notched frame on the first two shows and then abandoned it," Anderson says. "In the end, they were a little distracting, and we were probably the only ones who knew what was being referenced. Still, it was a nice little design moment for the brochure."

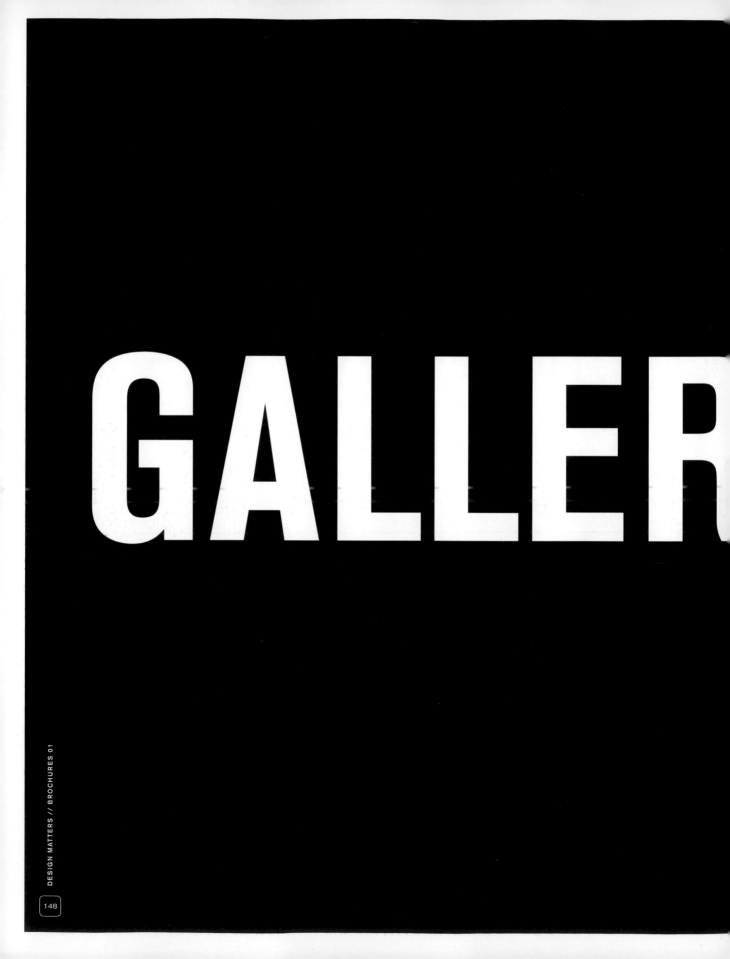

GALLER

Y

"I HAD A DINNER WITH A CLIENT, AND THE CLIENT SAID 'DO WE EVEN NEED TO PRODUCE AN ANNUAL REPORT NEXT YEAR?'" —DAVID SCHIMMEL, PRESIDENT AND CREATIVE DIRECTOR OF AND PARTNERS

HP Scitex
Industrial Wide Format Solutions

▲ *After Hewlett-Packard (HP) acquired Scitex, the industrial printer company needed to fold into its new owner's brand and visual identity. Jason & Jason, a design firm based in Israel, brought Scitex's corporate red into the updated look with permission from HP, creating a bridge between the old look and the new. These brochures were given out at trade shows.*

**Is it worth it?
Should we do it?
Why bother?**

**If the SEC says
you don't have to
deliver a printed
annual report,
who are we to say
you should?**

Here are **10 reasons** why we think it's a good idea.

◄▼ *"I had a dinner with a client, and the client said, 'Do we even need to produce an annual report next year?'"* says David Schimmel, president and creative director of And Partners in New York City. *"My stomach dropped."* Eventually, the conversation inspired this self-promotion piece, where the firm outlines all the reasons it believes a printed annual report is still a good idea.

Dear
Shareholders...

Dear
Potential investors...

Dear
Colleagues...

EVERYONE LISTENS

REALITY
PERCEPTION

ALIGNMENT

reason 2/10

Vision

*How well do investors know
your chairman?*

When executives speak in your
annual report, everyone listens.

It's an opportunity to evaluate
management's version of
your company's performance,
strategies and challenges.

reason 10/10

Perception vs. Reality

Your company's identity is within your
control. Its image—what others think—is
subject to all the noise of the marketplace.

The annual report can be the intersection
where perception and reality meet: the
most complete, specific, current utterance
of a public company's identity at a specific
point in time.

▲ In this brochure for professional-quality camera backs, Israeli design firm Jason & Jason used a spot UV lacquer to highlight individual photographs. This center spread features a testimonial from a fashion photographer and a series of black-and-white images to communicate the idea of rapid clicks.

►▼ *This piece belongs to a series of brochures that focus on employees at engineering company Walter P. Moore. As part of a rebranding effort, it told the firm's stories through current employees. "If you're going to rebrand the company, the place to start is your own people," says Thomas Hull, a principal at Rigsby Hull in Houston, Texas.*

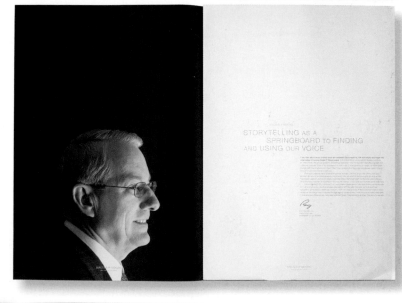

▲► *"Marc's a rebel,"* says Tim Hartford, president of Hartford Design in Chicago. *"I liked this idea of rule-breakers. Everyone in this book has that in common."* In this way, Marc Hauser's photos drove the concept for this promotional brochure about the photographer's work. This Uncle Sam spread, for example, features rules from an actual high school dress code.

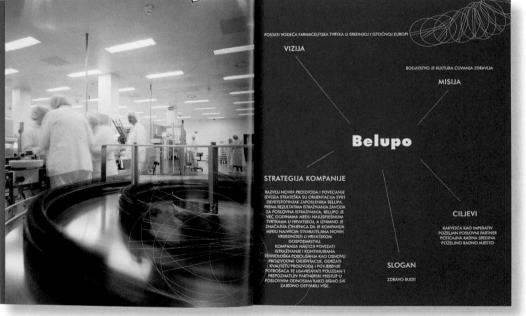

▲ *Studio Rašic designed this brochure
to promote one of Croatia's largest
pharmaceutical companies. The lower half
of the cover is varnished to suggest the
surface of a capsule. When readers open
the piece, the interior walks them through
the process for manufacturing a pill and
introduces them to the company that made it.*

CEMAL Sesleri duyuyor musun?
ŞAIR Evet, duyuyorum. Kadıköy meydanındayız...
Haziranın mutlu kuşları cıvıldıyor etrafta...
CEMAL İşçiler sel olmuş, akıyor. Ellerinde
pankartlar, bayraklar var, avazları çıktığı
kadar bağırıyorlar.

ŞAIR Sloganlar birbirine karışıyor, sağa sola
sinmiş polisler... Askerler barikat kurmuş...
Bekliyoruz... Birden kıyamet gibi bir çayırtı
koptu, kulağımın dibinden vınlayarak bir
kurşun geçti.
CEMAL Askerler ateş açtı, işçiler dört bir tarafa
kaçışmaya başladı. Ortalık fena karıştı,
binlerce insan ara sokaklarla dağıldı gitti.

◄▲ *Designer Esen Karol has worked with this independent theater company since 1995. The play promoted here is based on a novel about actual events that took place in Turkey before and after the country's military coup in 1980. To drive home the fictional play's links to the not-so-distant past, Karol ran historical images in black and white next to color shots from the play.*

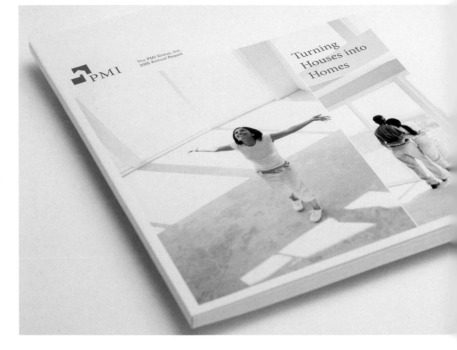

▶ ▼ *In this annual report, San Francisco's Fine Design Group helped The PMI Group put a face on mortgage insurance. The piece shows the kind of friendly people who benefit from the company's products, bringing out the human side of a financial business.*

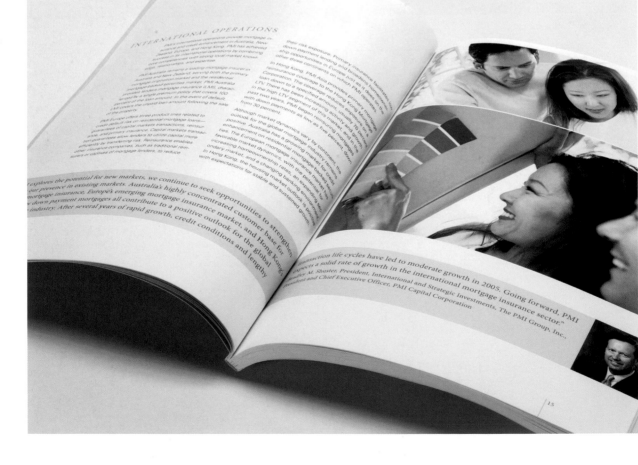

◄▼ *This marketing brochure, which was sent out with The PMI Group's annual report, features a Z-fold format that essentially creates two pieces in one. One cover and side promote the company's charity work, while the other highlights new products. For the latter, San Francisco's Fine Design Group shot original photography to communicate each concept. One of the spreads shown here plays off the old adage "don't put all your eggs in one basket" to illustrate a section on risk management.*

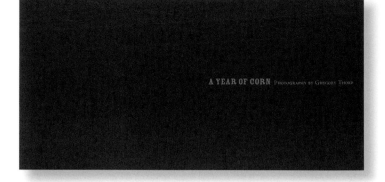

A YEAR OF CORN Photography by Gregory Thorp

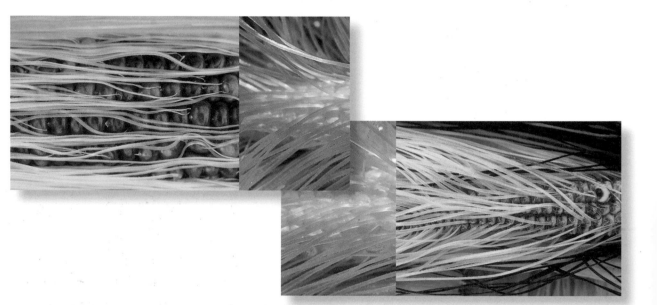

One day the treasure is form.
On another, the treasure is light.
On another, both.
This time it is night.

▲ *St. Louis design firm Kuhlmann Leavitt designed this book to promote the printing firm The Hennegan Company and showcase Gregory Thorp's photography. This book's small size makes flipping through the pages an intimate experience, while the uncoated, textured cover stock gives the piece an earthy feel.*

READY FOR OUR CLOSE-UP.

FEDERAL REALTY INVESTMENT TRUST
2006 ANNUAL REPORT

▲► *Lights, camera, action. For the Federal Realty Investment Trust's annual report, Hirshorn Zuckerman Design Group in Rockville, Maryland, played with a line from the classic movie* Sunset Boulevard. *The resulting cover line—"ready for our close-up"—influenced design decisions throughout the piece, such as using subtle film borders and presenting the management team as the ensemble cast.*

◄▼ *A small print run made it feasible for Minneapolis-based design firm Wink to include a range of production techniques within this brochure. The piece comes in a sleeve made from book board that's screen-printed with two colors. Tucked inside is a brochure that promotes the Marshall Field's department store to high-end jewelry vendors. In addition to being hand stitched, this piece features letterpress stickers to announce each section of the book.*

For this Sony brochure that was sent to retail stores, New York design firm Parham Santana wanted to reflect the lifestyles and interests of potential customers. The photography captures salient moments ranging from a child's birthday party to a vacation and little league game. A professional photographer took these images with Sony cameras.

Used by permission of Sony Electronics Inc.

Used by permission of Sony Electronics Inc.

Used by permission of Sony Electronics Inc.

► Rather than send clients a typical holiday card, the team at christiansen : creative in Hudson, Wisconsin, created this freestanding flip book to showcase the firm's humor. "People get inundated with the same thing, and we wanted to stand out," says creative director and owner Tricia Christiansen. This piece allows recipients to mix and match messages, with possibilities ranging from "eat snowflakes" to "celebrate puppies."

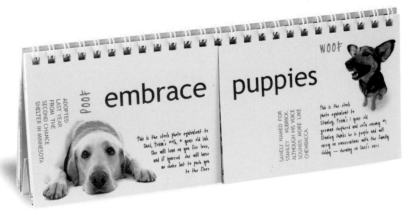

▼ *Christiansen : creative designed this brochure to promote redevelopment plans for The International Market Place, a retail area in Waikiki, Hawaii. Because the pages are stair-stepped, readers can view at least part of the full-color rendering from any section they're perusing.*

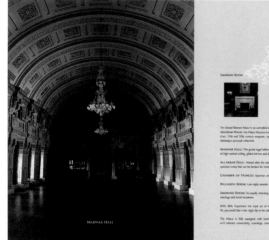

Umaid Bhawan Palace
Jodhpur, India

▲▶ *Shown here are two spreads and the cover jacket from a brochure promoting a luxury hotel located in a palace in India. "The concept was to successfully capture and present the bold Art Deco influences of the Umaid Bhawan Palace," says Divya Thakur, creative director at Design Temple in Mumbai.*

We license photographs.
Rights-protected photographs.
And hopefully, your photographs.

We do it in a way that you're probably not used to. You see...we're actually going to promote your photographs. That's right, they aren't going to sit forgotten on a website or in a book to gather dust like a jar of pickle relish. Our sales team is going to hit the street to get your work in front of our clients—who have a history of buying images. These are people who are looking for images that are unique. And more important, they're willing to pay top dollar to keep them that way.

And more clients?
We have about 22,000 of them.

We all know that the design world has become numbed by ordinary images. So let's show them the unexpected. We want to be your partner, your co-conspirator against the status quo. We're willing to give you as much or as little guidance as you need to do your best work. Why? Because we believe that your best work means your best shot at making more money. For you. For us. For everybody.

▲► *Planet Propaganda, based in Madison, Wisconsin, designed this brochure to help new stock agency UpperCut Images recruit top-notch photographers. Instead of images, the piece uses bold graphics and strong copy to capture attention.*

RESOU

RCES

"I HAD A PROFESSOR IN COLLEGE WHO WOULD CALL IT THE KISS. IT'S ONE LITTLE THING BEYOND WHAT'S EXPECTED, AND IT'S ALWAYS IN SERVICE OF THE PRODUCT." —TAMARA DOWD, CREATIVE DIRECTOR AT HIRSHORN ZUCKERMAN DESIGN GROUP

ASSOCIATIONS

AIGA
The professional association for design
www.aiga.org

The Art Directors Club
The forum for creativity in advertising, interactive
media and design
www.adcglobal.org

Color Marketing Group
An association for color design professionals
www.colormarketing.org

Icograda
The International Council of Graphic Design Associations
www.icograda.org

InSource
An association of corporate creatives
www.in-source.org

BLOGS

Another Limited Rebellion
Socially conscious design
www.alrdesign.com/blog

Designers Who Blog
A portal for design blogs
www.designers-who-blog.com

Design-Feed.net
A round up of highlights from other design blogs
www.design-feed.net

DesignNotes
Posts on culture, design and advertising
http://designnotes.info

Design Observer
Writings on design and culture
www.designobserver.com

The Laws of Simplicity/John Maeda
Design, business, technology, life
http://lawsofsimplicity.com

Speak Up
Graphic design conversation and dialogue
www.underconsideration.com/speakup

UnBeige
A blog about design
www.mediabistro.com/unbeige

BOOKS

*Ballsy: 99 Ways to Grow a Bigger Pair and Score
Extreme Business Success*
Karen Salmansohn
HOW Books

The Best of Brochure Design 9
Jason Godfrey
Rockport Publishers

Brochures: Making a Strong Impact
Jenny Sullivan
Rockport Publishers

Citizen Marketers: When People Are the Message
Ben McConnell and Jackie Huba
Kaplan Books

Color: Messages and Meanings
Leatrice Eiseman
Hand Books Press

The Creative Habit: Learn It and Use It for Life
Twyla Tharp
Simon & Schuster

Design Is: Words, Things, People, Buildings, and Places
Akiko Busch
Princeton Architectural Press

Getting It Right with Type: The Dos and Don'ts of Typography
Victoria Squire
Laurence King Publishing

Look at This: Contemporary Brochures, Catalogues, & Documents
Adrian Shaughnessy
Laurence King Publishing

Seventy-Nine Short Essays on Design
Michael Bierut
Princeton Architectural Press

Stylepedia: A Guide to Graphic Design Mannerisms, Quirks, and Conceits
Steven Heller and Louise Fili
Chronicle Books

Thinking with Type: A Critical Guide for Designers, Writers, Editors, & Students
Ellen Lupton
Princeton Architectural Press

MAGAZINES

Communication Arts
www.commarts.com

Dynamic Graphics
www.dynamicgraphics.com

Eye
www.eyemagazine.com

HOW
www.howdesign.com

I.D.
www.idonline.com

Metropolis
www.metropolismag.com

Print
www.printmag.com

STEP *inside design*
www.stepinsidedesign.com

WEBSITES

10 Ways
Visual language experiments
http://interact10ways.com

Creative Latitude
Education and business practices
www.creativelatitude.com

del.icio.us
A handy bookmarking tool
http://del.icio.us

The Design Encyclopedia
A user-built guide documenting design
www.thedesignencyclopedia.org

Dexigner
News and updates on a variety of design disciplines
www.dexigner.com

GigPosters
Work from top poster designers
www.gigposters.com

LinkedIn
Online networking for professionals
www.linkedin.com

BUTORS

"CONTENT IS KING." —THOMAS HULL,
PRINCIPAL AT RIGSBY HULL

ACTIA
France

Page 10, 12
Designer: Anne-Lise
Dermenghem

AND PARTNERS
USA
www.andpartnersny.com

Page 108, 109, 110, 111
Concept/design: And Partners,
NY
Creative director: David
Schimmel
Art director/designer:
Aimee Sealfon Eng
Designer: L. Megan Forb
Account executive:
Kristen Nagy
Content/writing: Walter
Thomas/Dewey Sadka
Client: Neenah Paper

Page 151
Creative director/designer:
David Schimmel
Designer: Eiji Tsuda
Copywriter: Michael Clive
Client: And Partners, NY

**ANOTHER LIMITED
REBELLION**
USA
www.ALRdesign.com

Page 71
Graphic design/illustration:
Noah Scalin

Page 77
Graphic design: Noah Scalin

**CHRISTIANSEN :
CREATIVE**
USA
www.christiansencreative.com

Page 164
Design and layout:
Tricia Christiansen

Page 165
Designer: Tricia Christiansen

**CINCINNATI CHILDREN'S
HOSPITAL MEDICAL
CENTER**
USA
www.cincinnatichildrens.org

Page 34
Art director: Andrea McCorkle
Designers: Nikki Mayhew,
Theresa Ryan
Copywriter/editor: Kate Harold
Printer: Wendling Printing
Company

Page 34
Experience Our Expertise
Art director/designer:
Andrea McCorkle
Copywriter/editor:
Monica Menke-Watts
Photographer:
Lyons Photography
Printer: Multi-Craft Litho, Inc.

Page 35
Art director/designer:
Andrea McCorkle
Copywriter/editor:
Monica Menke-Watts
Photographer: Greg Whitaker
Printer: Multi-Craft Litho, Inc.

Page 36
Art director/designer:
Andrea McCorkle
Copywriter/editor:
Monica Menke-Watts
Photographer: Greg Whitaker
Printer: Wendling Printing
Company

Page 37
Art director: Andrea McCorkle
Designers: Nikki Mayhew,
Theresa Ryan
Copywriter: Alison Momeyer
Editor: Monica Menke-Watts
Photographer:
Bronze Photography
Printer: Joseph Berning Printing
Company

CONNIE HWANG DESIGN
USA
www.conniehwangdesign.com

Page 112, 113
Design: Connie Hwang
Writer: Bethany Taylor
Client: University of Florida
School of Art and Art History
Printer: Alta Systems

Page 114, 115
Design: Connie Hwang
Writer: Amy Vigilante
Client: University Galleries
Printer: Fidelity Press

**THE DECODER RING
DESIGN CONCERN**
USA
www.thedecoderring.com

Page 40, 41
Design: Christian Helms
Copywriting: The Outfit,
Christian Helms

DESIGN ARMY
USA
www.designarmy.com

Page 8
Creative directors: Pum
Lefebure, Jake Lefebure
Designer: Mike Maluso
Copywriters: Claiken Tenglin,
Mike Maluso
Photographer: Max Hirshfield
Printer: Colorcraft of Virginia

Page 121, 122
Creative directors: Pum
Lefebure, Jake Lefebure
Designer: Dan Adler
Copywriter: Jim Bomemeier
Photographer: Thomas Arledge
Printer: Fannon Fine Printing

Page 123
Creative directors: Pum
Lefebure, Jake Lefebure
Designer: Lee Monroe
Copywriter: Jim Bomemeier
Illustrators: Tim Madle,
Lee Monroe
Printer: Fannon Fine Printing

DESIGN TEMPLE PVT. LTD.
India
www.designtemple.net

Page 166
Design and art direction: Divya
Thakur

ESEN KAROL DESIGN LTD.
Turkey

Page 124, 125, 126, 127
Design: Esen Karol
Copywriting: Esen Karol
Photography: Esen Karol

Page 156, 157
Design: Esen Karol
Performance photos: Ebru Bilun
Akyildiz

FINE DESIGN GROUP
USA
www.finedesigngroup.com

Page 132, 133, 134, 135
Design: FINE Design Group

Page 158, 159
Design: FINE Design Group

FLAT
USA
www.flat.com

Page 128, 129, 130, 131
Creative direction: Doug Lloyd
Art direction: Petter Ringbom
Design: Dan Arbello

Project management:
Laurel Ptak
Still-life photography:
Svend Lindback

GIAMPIETRO + SMITH
USA
www.studio-gs.com

Page 58, 59
Design: Giampietro + Smith

Page 104, 105, 106, 107
Design: Giampietro + Smith

HAHN SMITH DESIGN INC.
Canada
www.hahnsmithdesign.com

Page 13
Creative direction: Alison Hahn,
Nigel Smith
Designer: Derek Barnett
Copywriting: Barnaby
Southgate
Photography: Gibson & Smith,
Per Kristiansen, Brian Sano,
Bernard Prost
Client: Cuisipro

Page 24, 25
Creative direction: Alison Hahn,
Nigel Smith
Designer: Stéphane Monnet
Copywriting: Alison Hahn, Nigel
Smith, Stéphane Monnet
Photography: Bob Gundu,
Brian Sano
Client: Gourmet Settings

Page 26
Creative direction: Alison Hahn,
Nigel Smith
Designer: Dave Adams
Copywriting: Alison Hahn, Nigel
Smith, Paul Keyes, Herzig Eye
Institute
Photography: Matthew Plexman
Client: Herzig Eye Institute

Page 28
Creative direction: Alison Hahn,
Nigel Smith
Designer: Sara Soskolne
Copywriting: Nigel Smith, Sara
Soskolne, Abigail Pugh
Photography: Pete Patterson
Client: Gourmet Settings

HARTFORD DESIGN
USA
www.hartforddesign.com

Page 22, 23
Design director: Tim Hartford
Designer: Tim Hartford
Writer: Barbara Spier
Photography: Kipling Swehla
Printer: Reprox

Page 154
Design director: Tim Hartford
Designer: Tim Hartford
Photographer: Marc Hauser
Writer: Bob Bassi, Tim Hartford
Prepress and retouching:
Nimrod Systems
Printer: Segerdahl Graphics

**HIRSHORN ZUCKERMAN
DESIGN GROUP, INC.
(HZDG)**
USA
www.hzdg.com

Page 48
Executive creative director:
Karen Zuckerman
Creative director: Tamara Dowd
Art director: Jennifer Higgins

Page 51
Executive creative director:
Karen Zuckerman
Creative director: Tamara Dowd
Art director: Chris Walker

Page 53, 54
Executive creative director:
Karen Zuckerman
Creative director: Tamara Dowd
Art director: Jefferson Lui

Page 161
Executive creative director:
Karen Zuckerman
Creative director: Tamara Dowd
Art director: Leslie Harris

**HORNALL ANDERSON
DESIGN WORKS**
USA
www.hadw.com

Page 55
Design firm: Hornall Anderson
Design Works
Client: aishSeattle

Page 49
Design firm: Hornall Anderson
Design Works
Client: Eos Airlines

Page 47
Design firm: Hornall Anderson
Design Works
Client: Jobster

Page 46
Design firm: Hornall Anderson
Design Works
Client: Schnitzer Northwest

IRON DESIGN
USA
www.irondesign.com

Page 91
Design studio: Iron Design

Client: Tompkins County Area
  Development
Designer: Louis Johnson
Art director: Louis Johnson
Printer: Cayuga Press

**JASON & JASON VISUAL
COMMUNICATIONS**
Israel
www.jasonandjason.com

Page 30, 31
Art director: Jonathan Jason
Designer: Ilana Kotzin
Photography: Boudewin Staap

Page 150
Art director: Jonathan Jason
Designer: Ilana Kotzin

Page 152
Art director: Jonathan Jason
Designer: Michal Avrahami

KUHLMANN LEAVITT, INC.
USA
www.kuhlmannleavitt.com

Page 95
Design: Kuhlmann Leavitt

Page 141, 142, 143
Design: Kuhlmann Leavitt

Page 160
Design: Kuhlmann Leavitt
Photographer: Greggory Thorpe

LARSEN
USA
www.larsen.com

Page 89
Art director: Paul Wharton
Designer: Wendy Ruyle
Photographer: Nick Zdon
Writer: Diane Richard

Page 86
Art director: Paul Wharton
Designer: Liina Koukkari, Anna
  Giacomini, Bud Snead
Writer: Diane Richard

**LLOYDS GRAPHIC DESIGN
LTD.**
New Zealand

Page 97
Design: Lloyds Graphic Design
  Ltd.
Photography: Jim Tannock
  Photography

MADAME PARIS
France and Switzerland

Page 14, 15
Design: Madame Paris/Alex-
  andra Ruiz

PARHAM SANTANA INC.
USA
www.parhamsantana.com

Page 163
Creative director: John Parham
Design director: Emily Pak
Account director: Kelly McLees
Photographer: Frank Veronsky
Client: Sony Electronics Inc.

PLANET PROPAGANDA
USA
www.planetpropaganda.com

Page 136, 137, 138, 139, 167
Creative director: Kevin Wade
Senior designer: Travis Cain
Copywriter: Seth Gordon
Production designers: Evan
  Hartman, Ann Sweeney

PRINCIPLE
USA
www.designbyprinciple.com

Page 100, 101, 102, 103
Design: Allyson Lack, Jennifer
  Sukis, Pamela Zuccker
© 2007 Principle.
All rights reserved

RAND MCNALLY
USA
www.randmcnally.com

Page 78
Design: Julie Bastian

Page 77, 78
Design: Donna McGrath

RIGSBY HULL
USA
www.rigsbyhull.com

Page 27
Creative director: Lana Rigsby
Art director: Thomas Hull
Designers: Thomas Hull,
  Lana Rigsby
Photographer: Terry Vine

Page 153
Creative director: Lana Rigsby
Art director: Thomas Hull
Designers: Thomas Hull,
  Lana Rigsby
Photographer: Terry Vine
Writer: JoAnn Stone

ROVILLO + REITMAYER
USA
www.rovilloreitmayer.com

Page 93
Project: The Chiapas Project
Client: The Chiapas Project
Designer: Chris Rovillo
Photographer: Lucy Scott
Printer: Padgett Printing
Paper: Neenah Eames,
  Canvas and OKCO

Page 87, 88
Project: An Evening of
  Appreciation with Clint
  Eastwood
Client: Dallas Center for the
  Performing Arts
Designer: Kevin Thomas
Creative directors: Samantha
  Reitmayer, Chris Rovillo
Printer: Texas Graphic Resource
Paper: Neenah Eames,
  Architecture, Canvas and
  Furniture

Page 85
Project: RSVP Soirée
Client: RSVP Soirée
Designer: Emily Charette
Creative directors: Chris Rovillo,
  Samantha Reitmayer
Photographer: Christopher
  Porter
Printer: Allcraft Printing
Paper: Gilbert Esse,
  Productolith

RULE29 CREATIVE
USA
www.rule29.com

Page 74
Design: Rule29 Creative

Page 74, 75
Design: Rule29 Creative

SPOTCO
USA
www.spotnyc.com

Page 145, 146, 147
Creative director: Gail Anderson
Designer: Gary Montalvo
Photo producer: Mark Rheault
Photographer: Henry Leutwyler

STUDIO RAŠIC
Croatia
www.studio-rasic.hr

Page 155
Design: Ante Rašic,
  Lovorka Decker

Page 94
Design: Ante Rašic, Marko
  Rasic, Vedrana Vrabec

Page 11
Design: Ante Rašic,
  Lovorka Decker

TURNSTYLE
USA
www.turnstylestudio.com

Page 20, 21
Art director/designer: Ben
  Graham
Writer: Sally Bergesen
Client: Reebok

Page 70
Art director/designer: Steve
  Watson
Writer: Bruce Reynolds
Client: Steelcase Inc.

**URBANINFLUENCE
DESIGN STUDIO**
USA
www.urbaninfluence.com

VOICE
Australia
www.voicedesign.net

Page 116, 117
Art direction: Anthony Deleo,
  Scott Carslake
Design: Anthony Deleo
Typography: Anthony Deleo
Photography: Toby Richardson

Page 118, 119
Art direction: Scott Carslake,
  Anthony Deleo
Design: Scott Carslake
Typography: Scott Carslake
Photography: Toby Richardson

WINK
USA
www.wink-mpls.com

Page 162
Art directors: Scott Thares,
  Richard Boynton, Wink; Greg
  Clark, Marshall Fields
Designer: Scott Thares
Illustrator: Scott Thares
Copywriter: Adam Reynolds,
  Marshall Fields
Photography: Marshall Field's
  Historical Archives
Client: Marshall Fields

About the Author

Michelle Taute is a writer and editor based in Cincinnati. She writes about graphic design for a wide range of magazines, including *HOW*, STEP *inside design*, and *Dynamic Graphics*. Her articles have also appeared in a wide variety of national magazines including *Better Homes and Gardens, Woman's Day Special Interest Publications, USA Weekend, Metropolis, Natural Home,* and *The Writer.*

Before her days as a freelancer, Taute worked on the editorial teams of an eclectic list of national magazines. Those titles include *I.D., The Artist's Magazine, Family Tree* magazine, *Decorative Artist's Workbook, Popular Woodworking*—and even a stint on a short-lived Bob Ross magazine. She continues to take on content editing and project management duties for magazines and books. In addition to editorial work, she regularly handles copywriting for major consumer brands.

www.michelletaute.com